WE'VE BEEN ROBBED

WE'VE BEEN ROBBED!

or

A Dispensationalist Looks at the Baptism of the Holy Spirit

by

Wilfrid C. Meloon

Logos International

Plainfield, N.J.

Standard Book Number: 912106-19-0
Library of Congress Catalog Card Number: 70-166500
Logos, International, Plainfield, N.J. 07060
©1971 by Logos, International. All rights reserved.
Printed in the United States of America.

TABLE OF CONTENTS

PREFACE

The church today has been robbed.
Robbed of its credentials: miracles, signs, and wonders.
Robbed of its power: the Holy Spirit baptism.
Robbed of its emphasis: anointed ministries.

The return of the miracle ministry through the contemporary emphasis on the baptism of the Holy Spirit in churches of all denominations proves that it is possible for the Holy Spirit to work among the believers through signs and wonders as God promised (Mark 16:17-20; Heb. 2:3-4) without the errors, abuses, and excesses that have been the basis of criticism in the past.

After years of being a fundamentalist preacher I have arrived at the conclusion that the intricate system contrived about 150 years ago, popularized by John Darby's commentaries and the *Scofield Reference Bible* and perpetrated by a large number of "fundamentalists," has consistently robbed the church of much needed power and has been used to justify the absence of the supernatural in our ministries.

But fundamentalism and these ministries are not incompatible. Indeed, they should support one another. Fundamentalism's number one bedrock thesis, that the Bible is the Word of God, is the basis of my entire plea in this presentation.

I do not advocate the abrogation of the whole dispensational system. I simply plead for back-to-the-Bible changes which will restore the positive teaching of the early church distinctions of miracles, signs, and wonders as effective in the winning of precious souls to Christ through a revived church.

God is still alive and well. Only some of His people are "dead."

And His church is sick—nigh unto death. I have ministered

for some thirty years to these sick churches in an altogether too weak ministry myself. Now, however, a deeper experience with the Holy Spirit, inspired by observation of what is happening, has put a "woe" into my preaching, a hope into my teaching, and an "I've got it!" into my philosophy. I'm glad to be numbered among the "in crowd"—"in," that is, the "charismatic renewal."

Dry bones are beginning to rattle once again; they are "coming together," climbing denominational walls, and "life" is beginning to appear in the sinews of the visible church. Ah! We are "stretching every nerve." Shackles of doctrinal bondage lie broken all over the battlefield, and "new" Christians are running with the gospel to the unsaved, and with news of the Spirit's outpouring to the born again.

Many a charismatic theologian has lifted his pen to tell his experience, to spread the printed page, broadcast the fires, and scatter the light. But few have delved into the doctrinal controversies aroused. My aim is to give the "renewal" a sound doctrinal footing, for there must be a balance between "experience" and "the Word."

May God use this contribution!

CHAPTER I

SOMETHING'S WRONG!

You see, Jesus Christ told us to evangelize this world. He said, "Go ye into all the world and preach the gospel" and "Go ye therefore, and teach all nations." Yet He preceded His commands with a promise of endowment with power: "All power is given unto me in heaven and in earth"; and "Behold, I send the promise of my Father upon you." A little later He said, "Ye shall be baptized with power and the Holy Ghost," and "Ye shall receive power after that the Holy Ghost is come upon you."

But it has been nearly 2000 years since then, and instead of gaining on the world, the world is far outnumbering the believers in every generation. Our effectiveness, as a church, seems null and void. We lack authority (power) and energy (power). Spokesmen for the visible church are instead wrapped up in social endeavor, civil rights, draft card burning, and even civil disobedience.

Something's wrong!

There are 324,000 babies born every day. Each of them is a potential convert to Christ. Some 133,000 people die every day. Thus the population increase is more than 190,000 daily. Yet of these, less than one out of a hundred will become a Christian.

Let's Face the Issues!

Does the Christian church measure up to this challenge? What are we doing about it? Are we "communicating" at all? We seem all too interested in maintaining the *status quo* (that's Latin for "the mess we're in").

We sing, "Like a mighty army, moves the church of God."

At a snail's pace.

"We're marching to Zion!" Yes, like we are going to a funeral.

"To the work, to the work!" Yet we're really just playing church.

"Stand up, Stand up for Jesus!"

"Sure, man, but let's not get fanatic about it. It's easier to sit on the premises than to stand on the promises."

I figured it out one day. Where I live in Orange County, Florida, each of our 200 churches would have to have 26 converts every week just to keep up with the population explosion. Considering the many churches who don't believe in "conversions" and don't give invitations, every evangelical church's portion would be much higher than that. But how many conservative churches gain that many a year? The world goes merrily on its way to hell, while we play church, raise money, erect million-dollar edifices called "Houses of God." Here we sing somber songs attracting no one and recite prayers that don't even reach the ceiling.

We start our services with, "The Lord is in His Holy Temple," but we see little evidence of His visit—no power, no signs, no wonders, no miracles. It reminds me of the legendary story of an old man climbing the steps of a fashionable city church in his ragged clothes. Two sentinels barred the door and asked why he wanted to enter the church.

"To worship the Lord," the old man replied.

They stalled him off: "Why don't you go home and pray about whether you should come to this church or not."

He agreed, but the next Sunday was seen climbing the long steps again. "Did you do what we said?" the sentinels asked.

"I did," he replied.

"Well, what did God tell you when you prayed about coming to this church?"

"He told me, 'Keep trying, son. I've been trying to get into that church for more'n twenty years myself.'"

"Let all the earth keep silence," the choir softly drones, when I feel like SHOUTING, "Glory to God, I'm saved! I'm healed! I'm filled with His Spirit!" Why should I keep silence before Him? Souls need to come to Christ, and yet I'm told to whisper the gospel—as if I'm scared to death. "Awake, thou that sleepest, and arise from the dead, and Christ shall give thee light!" (Eph. 5:14).

So, the church is lulled to sleep as though her songs were lullabies and her "gos-pill" were tranquilizers. Of course, there are many "spiritual sedatives." There are many sources of somnambulism which have entered into the church or which have worked on it from without; but I can think of no greater cause of the church's weakness today than the subtle facetiousness of one of its own great bulwarks—DISPENSATIONALISM.

And among evangelicals, that's the issue!

CHAPTER II

LET'S TRACK IT DOWN!

I was recently interviewed on a Christian television program entitled "Charisma." "Why is it that so many Baptists, especially Independent Baptists like yourself, do not accept the gifts of the Spirit as for today?" I was asked.

I answered as I have so many times in the past thirty years: "It is not a matter of denominationalism, but a matter of dispensationalism."

"But," the interviewer commented, "you implied that this is the bulwark of your faith."

This may seem like an anachronism, but let me explain. In the early 1800's the church saw the rise and spread of postmillennialism. The people of God were lulled into an attitude of "waiting for the Kingdom" to come to earth. They proclaimed, "We are in the millennium now. The church is getting stronger and stronger. We've created the Kingdom of God on earth, and soon Christ will come to be our king."

This amazing bit of self-exalting sophistry led the church into an era of "sleep walking" instead of "soul winning." To offset this trend, a strong fundamental dispensationalism arose with the writings of John Darby and others.

However, the cure turned out to be almost as deadly as the disease; for dispensationalism gave us an eschatology (doctrine of last things) and a pneumatology (doctrine of the Holy Spirit) which completely ruled out the power of the Holy Spirit in these latter days as far as the New Testament pattern of the supernatural is concerned—a theology which now needs serious reevaluation in the light of the burgeoning charismatic renewal. However, lest I bore you with big words, I simply mean that it is high time we faced up to why we are so powerless.

The whole matter can be summed up in three words: WE'VE BEEN ROBBED. Dispensationalists compartmentalize the scriptures, like a postman sorting our mail. Each little word or promise has to be put in just the right box (dispensation), and they forbid anyone to take any promise out of one box and put it in another.

The sheer weight of C.I. Scofield daring to put his comments between the covers of his *Scofield Reference Bible* has duped countless sincere Christians into believing that his theological theories are of equal inspiration with the Word itself. "But there can be no such thing as healings, miracles and tongues now," the lay theologian will say desperately as he shakes his Scofield Bible in your face; "see, it says so right here in the Bible." And then he places his quivering finger on the marginal comments of Scofield.

In a nutshell, dispensationalism teaches that the history of the world has been divided into seven "dispensations" or "period[s] of time during which man is tested in respect to his obedience to some specific revelation of the will of God." [1] These seven dispensations are aligned with the Letters to the Seven Churches as recorded in the first three chapters of the Revelation. Students of this system of theology say we are now in the last dispensation, that of Laodicea ("lukewarmness"). It is easy to see how this rose up in opposition to the postmillennial theory that we were getting better and better every day in every way.

"No," the dispensationalist said, "just the very opposite; we are getting worse and worse every day, and eventually things will get so bad that the Lord will come again, ushering in His Kingdom." I am not at all in disagreement with this basic theory, but I am in disagreement with any theory that compartmentalizes the Scripture and therefore rules out the power of God for this age. And that is exactly what dispensationalism has done.

The Book of Acts is looked upon today by all too many in the church as history only. The book is really the acts of the Holy Spirit as well as the acts of the Apostles. "Apostolic succession" is a doctrine in disrepute, but actually there is no

[1]C.I. Scofield, ed. *The New Scofield Reference Bible* (New York: Oxford Univ. Press, 1967), p. 3.

scriptural evidence whatsoever to indicate the abrogation of this office. An "apostle" is "one sent," but most church offices today aren't worth "two cents." (Pardon the pun.) Without the power, the office is vacant indeed. Yet few deny that Acts is our pattern, our blueprint for revival and success in carrying out the great commission.

J. Morgan words it this way:

"The day of Pentecost is a model of the work in the church today. It formed the opening scene of the new dispensation. By an example it gave the world to know and understand what was meant by the ministration of the Holy Spirit of which it was the commencement. O, that the world had continued as it was then begun! So long as Pentecostal times lasted, the church was extended, large inroads were made everywhere on the kingdom of darkness. . . . We are encouraged to hope that Pentecostal effusions shall again visit the world. . . . No doubt, there are people to whom all such things will appear vain and foolish but we must not be stumbled by them. There were such on the day of Pentecost. Three classes are mentioned by the historian: some were "amazed," looking at the work with mere curiosity and surprise. Others were 'in doubt,' filled with skepticism and suspicion. And not a few, mocking said, 'These men are full of new wine.' So it was then and it is well we are informed of it. There are those whom no evidence would satisfy and no truth convince. We must not be discouraged by the lukewarmness nor deterred by the irreligion of others." [2]

Lukewarmness. John R. Rice calls this the sin that makes God vomit. The only antidote for this disease is power. And power comes only through the baptism of the Holy Spirit. Yet it is this experience that the dispensationalist says is no longer valid today. You see, we've been robbed.

Because of this robbery, the church triumphant has become the church reticent. The church visible has become the church inaudible. Destined for power, we are eaten up with palsy. The church has become a laughingstock. We are chuckled at, ridiculed to scorn for our "pinkpill" gospel, the formal liturgy, pompous rituals, liberal theology, feeble

[2] J. Morgan, *The Scripture Testimony to the Holy Spirit* (Edinburgh: T.&T. Clark, 1865).

message, and sociocentric religiosity. On the other side, people are berated with a negative message that has far more overtones of being "bad news" than "good news." There are a million things to preach against, but because the miraculous, the supernatural, has been removed from our midst, we find very little to testify for.

Two men stood by a burning down church one night. Suddenly they recognized each other and one quipped, "Well, this is the first time I have ever seen you out to church."

The other replied, "This is the first time I've seen this church on fire."

Yet we cringe at the words of conviction, "These signs shall follow them that believe ... " until some theologian explains, "These verses were not in the original manuscript." Then we can sigh with relief. Jesus said, "They shall speak with new tongues," and yet many of today's preachers pooh-pooh the charismatic renewal as "all of Satan." Insecurity causes many pastors to downgrade the natural inquisitiveness of their flocks who thirst and hunger after the "rivers of living water" and the "bread of life." They dismiss the growing tide of interest in the charismata as "mere fanaticism."

But what about these signs, gifts, and wonders? Did God *take* them away? Can it be His fault that the church is bereft of these powers?

Someone says, "But God doesn't work that way today." If this is your argument, then it is because of the impressions of dispensationalism you have picked up somewhere along the line.

I am not advocating the demise of dispensationalism but rather changes from within. Just as it has undergone changes in the century and a half it has been alive in our midst, so dispensationalism needs further changes today.

What was taught to me twenty-five years ago as just plain "dispensationalism" is, in the eyes of Ryrie, Walvoord, English, and others "ultradispensationalism" now. Large segments of historical dispensationalism are now repudiated as the system mellows, changed by the procession of exponents down through the years. This is precisely what I am advocating—a further changing which will, in its fundamentalism, include the Biblical emphasis of a supernatural ministry and miraculous results.

Why don't we have that element of miracle now in the churches that believe in dispensationalism? R.A. Torrey, famed evangelist and longtime associate of Dwight L. Moody says:

"This (the baptism of the Holy Spirit) is a matter of great practical importance for there are many who are not enjoying the fullness of privilege that they might enjoy because by pushing individual verses in the scripture beyond what they will bear and against the plain teachings of the scripture as a whole they are trying to persuade themselves that they have already been baptized with the Holy Spirit when they haven't, and if they would only admit to themselves that they have not, they could then take the steps whereby they would be baptized with the Holy Spirit as a matter of definite experience." [3]

This is the trouble with the dispensational system as it now exists. We need the teaching as Torrey taught it in his day. The sad part is, we have to go back into history to find quotations like these of Spirit-filled men among fundamentalist ranks.

Although I do not agree with all Philip Mauro says, he did put his finger on the problem when he said:

"Indeed the time is fully ripe for a thorough examination and frank exposure of this new and subtle form of modernism that has been spreading itself among those who have adopted the name 'fundamentalist.' For evangelical Christianity must purge itself of this leaven of dispensationalism ere it can display its former power and exert its former influence." [4]

Whatever else may be said of dispensationalists, they are not liberal in doctrine. I agree with them on the fundamentals—the total inspiration of the scriptures, the doctrine of the trinity, the deity of Christ, His sinless life, His perfect substitutionary sacrifice on the cross, His shed blood spilled

[3] R.A. Torrey, *The Person and Work of the Holy Spirit* (Chicago: Revell, 1910).

[4] Philip Mauro, *The Gospel of the Kingdom* (Boston: Hamilton Bros., 1928) pp. 8-9.

for our sins, His literal return to this earth, visible and in bodily form. But I also agree with Mauro that concerning some scriptures, their system is as effective as modernism in getting rid of the power of God from the Bible.

This is the core of their adamant stand against the Book of Acts as the pattern for today. The dispensationalist says, "As history Acts is accurate, but as a pattern for the church today it is pure fanaticism."

Daniel Fuller, son of Charles E. Fuller of the famed "Old-Fashioned Revival Hour," says of dispensationalism, that it is " . . . internally inconsistent and unable to harmonize itself with the Biblical data . . . " [5]

Many other voices are being lifted against this system as much because of its eschatology (doctrine of last things) as because of its pneumatology (doctrine of the Holy Spirit). But it all amounts to the fact that we've been robbed.

I know this is a deliberately sensational statement, but my purpose is to drive readers to examine their Bibles on this matter rather than read other books or listen to proponents of various theological systems. The great missionary George Mueller once said:

"My brother, I am a constant reader of my Bible, and I soon found out that what I was taught to believe did not always agree with what my Bible said. I came to see that I must either part company from John Darby, or from my precious Bible, and I chose to cling to my Bible and part from Mr. Darby." [6]

The same dispensationalism gives us innumerable resurrections, at least two second comings of Christ, a secret pre-tribulation rapture of the church, evangelization of the world by the Jews (saved by some unrevealed gratuitous miracle) during the last seven years between the two second comings, and a tribulation period without the Holy Spirit to achieve a task which the church has been commissioned to do for 2000 years WITH THE HOLY SPIRIT. A man could read his Bible for a hundred years and never find such a ridiculous plan, and yet because men like Darby and Scofield put it into

---

[5] From an unpublished doctoral dissertation.
[6] Alexander Fraser, *The Return of Christ in Glory* (Scottdale, Pa.: The Evangelical Fellowship, Inc., 1943), p. 69.

print, millions have been duped into following this system, rather than the clear teachings of the Word of God.

Perhaps you would be interested to know how a great man like Dwight L. Moody felt about the baptism of the Holy Spirit which today's dispensationalists say is of the devil. Listen to the words of R.A. Torrey:

"Once he (Moody) had some teachers at Northfield, fine men all of them, but they did not believe in a definite Baptism with the Holy Ghost for the individual. They believed that every child of God was baptized with the Holy Ghost, and they did not believe in any special Baptism with the Holy Ghost for the individual. Mr. Moody came to me and said, 'Torrey, will you come up to my house after the meeting tonight and I will get these men to come, and I want you to talk this thing out with them.' Of course I readily consented, and Mr. Moody and I talked for a long time, but they did not altogether see eye to eye with us. And when they went, Mr. Moody signaled me to remain for a few minutes. Mr. Moody sat there with his chin on his breast, as he often sat when in deep thought; then he looked up and said, 'Oh, why will they split hairs? Why don't they see that this is just the one thing that they themselves need? They are good teachers, they are wonderful teachers, and I am so glad to have them here; but why will they not see that the Baptism with the Holy Ghost is just the one touch that they themselves need?' " [7]

But, ah, the tragedy! These men, "fine men, all of them" had been robbed by a system that Moody almost wholly ignored.

[7] R.A. Torrey, *Why God Used D.L. Moody* (Chicago: Moody Press, 1923) p. 59-60.

CHAPTER III

WHAT IS DISPENSATIONALISM?

In his book, *Dispensationalism Today,* Ryrie says, "It is granted that as a system of theology dispensationalism is recent in origin."[1]

As a system, dispensationalism was largely formulated by John Darby around 1825. To justify the system Ryrie said:

"The fact that the church taught something in the first century does not make it true. And likewise, if the church did not teach something until the twentieth century it is not necessarily false."[2]

Think that one through, fundamentalists. No wonder Mauro evaluated their system as a "subtle form of modernism." If we accept Ryrie's statement, then dispensationalism is a far more effective tool for robbing the church than the modernist who conveniently clips passages out of the canon with his liberal scissors. The liberal is obvious; the dispensationalist is devious.

Ryrie says, "The essence of dispensationalism is (1) the recognition of a distinction between Israel and the church, (2) a consistently literal principle of interpretation, and (3) a basic and working conception of the purpose of God as his own glory rather than as the single purpose of salvation."[3] These are three basic working principles of this theological system which is robbing the church. Anyone who uses this system, who embraces this dispensational framework or mold, must abide by these three preconceived tenets as a basis for all Bible study. Into this dispensational mold

[1] Charles C. Ryrie, *Dispensationalism Today* (Chicago: Moody, 1965), p. 67.

[2] *Ibid.*

[3] *Ibid.,* p. 48.

everything has to fit, and any Biblical truth that doesn't, must be twisted until it does.

What Does This Lead To?

Ryrie says, "The dispensationalist finds his answer to the need for distinctions in his dispensational scheme."[4] Notice, he *finds* his answer, inplying a search. The search is obviously necessary when he reads the Book of Acts and sees the early church on the march and compares it with the church stripped of all possibility of miracle by this "scheme." He sees Peter preach one sermon resulting in 3,000 souls saved, but then must painfully remind himself that today's church is full of preachers who weekly grind out 3,000 sermons to every soul that's saved. He sees the gifts of the Spirit, the fruit of the Spirit, the power of the Spirit and has to admit that the contemporary church does not have them now. How much easier it is to justify the lack of power through a theological system than to cry out to God admitting weakness.

The fledgling student of theology, listening to these false teachings, nods in understanding. "So, no wonder we don't have these things today; we're not supposed to have them." He smiles, sighs, his soul calm within him. And the rise of desire, the spurt of enthusiasm that comes from the challenge of the Spirited early church, is quenched. The fire is deluged by the cold hard facts of accepted theology. He has been robbed by dispensationalism and doesn't know it.

I have always considered myself a dispensationalist. Ryrie in quoting Chafer says, "There is some truth in the statements that any person is a dispensationalist who trusts the blood of Christ rather than bringing an animal sacrifice and any person is a dispensationalist who observes the first day of the week rather than the seventh."[5] Chafer's words sound reasonable and more brotherly than Ryrie's categorical denial of anyone in his camp unless they believe what Ryrie calls the "three essentials of dispensationalism." What I must take a stand against is the system that robs us of the promise of

[4] *Ibid.*, p. 16.

[5] *Ibid.*

God concerning the work and ministry of the Holy Spirit.

Do I need to approach a passage of scripture which presents a problem and say to myself, "Now in order to understand this verse, I must remember I am a fundamentalist or dispensationalist. Therefore, this scripture *can't* mean this or that"? It is the same as approaching the Bible as a racist; having first conceived the notion that God is a segregationist, it therefore becomes easy to "prove" your doctrinal stand with scripture—that is, if you don't mind bending a few passages and "interpreting" a few others.

This is wrong hermeneutics. Any system of interpretation will bind the serious student of God's Word to a rut. Believe the Bible for just what it says; simply accept what it teaches; try to understand what it means; and let the chips fall where they may. What people "tag" you really doesn't matter. Give the Holy Spirit His place in understanding the Bible; after all, He wrote it.

Personally, I am loath to give up the designation of dispensationalist, if designated I must be. But terms mean little these days; tags are profuse and profane sometimes. Yet for those who wonder, I here and now testify to being a firm fundamentalist, a concerned conservative, an evangelistic evangelical, a practicing premillennialist, and a strong separationist.

Twenty-five years of my life has been spent as an evangelist, pastor, and missionary. My wife and I have traveled the eastern half of the United States and Canada in churches of all denominations, preaching, singing, playing our instruments. As an Independent Baptist I speak out strongly against formalism, inclusivism, unholy alliances, modernism, liberalism, and ecumenicity. I've authored several booklets against worldliness. [6] I have conducted large evangelistic campaigns, many regular radio programs, television programs of my own and as a guest, and in all of this, through thirty years I have noticed that just as soon as anyone embraces certain Biblical truths that are contrary to the dispensational establishment, he is branded as "modernist," "liberal," "fanatic," or even "communist." This has been the experience of many fine

[6] Wilfrid C. Meloon, *Hey, Young People: They Say I Am Crazy!* (Murfreesboro, Tenn.: Sword of the Lord, 1956) and Meloon, *Old Nic Loses a Customer* (Cleveland, Ohio: Union Gospel Press, 1949).

Christian workers who have finally thrown off the yoke of this system. Feeling themselves no longer slaves to what their alma maters drubbed into them, they have taken the Bible at face value, found new experiences in the Holy Spirit's power, and their ministries have been renovated. Sometimes they were ostracized from their group, excommunicated from their church, or denied denominational standing. Their "new views" drove them to new pastures.

I've quoted from some "old-timers" and will again, but look with me at one contemporary. Pat Boone, the famous singer and teen-age idol, gives a glowing testimony in his new autobiography, *A New Song*. [7] Himself a preacher, supplying pulpits in his denomination for years, he grew cold to a powerless church, and with his wife almost departed from the faith. My point of interest is the comparison he draws between what his church taught him and what he now has been compelled to believe.

After telling in no uncertain terms what he now believes the Bible teaches plainly about the baptism in the Holy Spirit and speaking in tongues, he says, "I'd taught her myself (my wife) the 'church position' on the gifts of the Spirit, listed in I Cor. 12. We believed that when the beloved apostle John, exiled on the Isle of Patmos, wrote the last words of the Revelation, and God's Word was completed, that miraculous or supernatural gifts of the Holy Spirit ceased. They weren't needed anymore." [8] Boone finally admits that there was so much scripture about something that "ended in the first century" that he finally had to hurdle all dispensational dogmas. After his wife's baptism in the Spirit some well-meaning minister friend was talking with her and suddenly stooped, cupped the chin of their little girl in his hands, and said, "Honey, don't let your momma make a nun of you."

These "robbers." They stir my irascibilities to a boiling point! Shocked and hurt, Pat's wife told him, "I don't think I will pray in my new language anymore." She even felt that her experience might have been some "satanic, mystic trip," all because of the thoughtless words of a "man of God" who was trying to be funny to cover up for his own powerlessness.

[7] Pat Boone, *A New Song* (Carol Stream, Ill.: Creation House, 1970).

[8] *Ibid.*, p. 107.

"You aren't going to let the uninformed intellect of one well-meaning young minister rob you of what the Lord Himself has given you, are you?" Pat asked her. She shook her head, but it had robbed her temporarily. And just think of the many who have been robbed not just temporarily, but permanently.

Pat Boone's experience (and that of the "five women in his life") surely testifies to the falsity of the dispensational dogma. The Boones needed the "prayer language." They needed that "something extra" that only the baptism in the Spirit could supply. They were almost on the rocks morally and spiritually, heading for divorce; they needed Him.

And who doesn't? As a result of Boone's testimony, many young lives have been influenced for Christ; young people have been baptized in his backyard Beverly Hills swimming pool. Boone, like so many others who go contrary to the dispensational system, has, at this writing, just been "excommunicated" from his Church of Christ denomination. But his latest album, "Rapture," is enjoying success, even greater than some of his songs of the world when he was entertaining only. Now you don't get this kind of thing from dispensationalism and all its spiritual "no-nos."

Pentecostalism vs. the Charismatic Renewal

There is no such thing as a Pentecostal denomination, any more than there is a Baptist denomination. There are more Baptists than you can shake a stick at, and most of them need a *big* stick shaken at them. The various Pentecostal groups differ, however, from the newer charismatic renewal movements, although there are things in common to both groups. Modern Pentecostalism is somewhere close to 100 years old, having its rise in the Welsh revival and in others like the one in Hot Springs, Arkansas, and the Azusa Street prayer meetings in California. The charismatic renewal is quite recent as a movement, and defies description as to the origin or originator.

Among the Pentecostal groups, believing strongly in the ministry of the "sign-gifts" and the miraculous in general, there are some who still cling to "dispensationalism" as a system. They ardently teach eschatology from Larkin's chats, almost worship the Scofield Bible, and dispensationalize almost everything—except the Holy Spirit. This poses a problem. How can they be so inconsistent? It doubtless stems from the fact that this system of eschatology (the present system of dispensational premillennialism) was the position of their founder, Edward Irving. This system includes such theories as the pre-tribulation rapture, Jewish evangelism during the tribulation period, a Jewish "complexion" to the millennium that almost excludes the church, multiple resurrections instead of the two the Bible teaches, a second and third coming of Christ (they call it "split phase" of one coming) with the rapture and the revelation as two separate events in time with seven years between them (some say three and a half).

The eminent S.P. Tragelles points out that Edward Irving once had a vision of this whole system of prophetic understanding. He began preaching it, and the scholars of the day, enamored of the scheme, started hunting scriptures to support it. This was the birth of the "dispensational" prophetic scheme. And through the twisting and warping of the scriptures, eschatology as a study lost its true Biblical basis. Thus while dispensationalism robbed fundamentalists of their rightful power through the Holy Spirit, this same insidious doctrine was used by Pentecostal leaders to rob them of the meaning of prophecy.

We shall not speak here of the personal lives of either Darby or Irving, who were bitter enemies at times, for we do not feel as some do that their personal lives are evidence of the truth or falsehood of their teaching. Suffice it to say, neither of them has a very enviable record along some lines.

It is strange, though, that one should be desirous of being known as a "Pentecostal" and a "dispensationalist" at the same time. The two terms are quite incompatible. It is like being a "Republican Democrat" or a "black white man" or a "brave coward."

Lest I be misunderstood, I challenge each reader who may be under the yoke of dispensationalism to forsake it and get his theology from the Bible. Someone has said, "There is nothing new under the sun except that which is false." Therefore, go back to your Bibles. If the Bible does not teach a pre-tribulation rapture, why believe it? If the Bible does not clearly state, "These gifts of the Spirit passed away because the Bible is completed and we no longer need them," then don't believe they did. Believe the Bible! Claim its promises! Receive the gifts!

CHAPTER IV

DISPENSATIONALISM AND THE HOLY SPIRIT

What does dispensationalism do to the doctrine and consequently to the ministry of the Holy Spirit today?

Dr. John F. Walvoord is probably the foremost spokesman today for dispensationalism, along with Charles Ryrie, both of Dallas Theological Seminary. Although we could quote endless material on the Holy Spirit by dispensationalists, let us use Walvoord's textbook, *The Holy Spirit,* [1] as a basis. It, along with Ryrie's book, fairly equalizes and summarizes the average position of dispensational theology today.

As I first picked up Walvoord's book, I read the jacket introduction as follows: "This volume on the third person of the trinity is . . . " Now, who says that the Holy Spirit is the "third" person of the Trinity? Dr. Walter Wilson has rightly protested, "The Holy Spirit will take third place to nobody." You'll never find the Holy Spirit referred to as the "third person of the trinity" in the scriptures, nor will you find Christ referred to as the second person. They are all three coexistent and coequal. They are God, one God, eternally existent in three persons. *This is fundamental.* How can we refer to them as first, second, and third?

Tragically, most people are far more enamored of a system of preconceived, self-imposed principles of hermeneutics than they are of the real meanings and the total message of the Bible.

"Doctrine by implication is a valid means of Bible study," I recently heard a dear pastor say. I gulped! I waited for someone to object.

But no one did.

They swallowed this bit of human sophistry because it is

[1]John F. Walvoord, *The Holy Spirit* (Wheaton, Ill.: Van Kampen, 1954).

part and parcel of the dispensational system. It has to be, or they could never come up with some of their focal points in the system of teaching which is accepted as "gospel" today.

Do we need any "doctrine" which can be "backed up" only by implication?

Walvoord says, "A serious departure from the truth is found in the attempt by some of the holiness movements to link the Baptism of the Spirit with certain temporary spiritual gifts and their exercises."[2] The first question that comes to mind is, "Who says what gifts are temporary?" What gifts are permanent and why? Walvoord continues, "It is clear that the great body of Bible-loving Christians does not have all the spiritual gifts manifested in its midst as did the early apostolic church. On the other hand, certain gifts clearly characterize the entire present dispensation."[3] The implication is plain: *because we do not have them, we are not supposed to have them.* This is the "argument from silence" propagated first by Sir Robert Anderson, an ultradispensationalist according to the party line today.

When I went to Bible Institute I was taught that after Pentecost there was a "transition period," which was a separate dispensation. In addition to the separate dispensation for the apostolic times, there was a separate dispensational period for the "tribulation" period after the rapture. Today such teaching would be tagged as ultradispensational. The modern dispensationalism using the terminology of "temporary gifts" and "permanent gifts" have as effectively robbed us as the earlier teachings of Gray, Gaebelein, Haldeman, Ironsides, Pettingill, Anderson, Blackstone, Scofield, Chafer, DeHaan, and others.

Look At The Gifts

Walvoord says, "Certain gifts are clearly the possession of the church today as exhibited in their exercise in gifted men throughout the present dispensation. . . . In contrast to these as their individual exposition will demonstrate, stand other spiritual gifts known by the early Christians, which seem to

[2] *Ibid.,* p. 139.
[3] *Ibid.,* p. 167.

have passed from the scene with the apostolic period. . . . Among these temporary gifts the following can be named: (1) the gift of apostleship, (2) the gift of prophecy, (3) the gift of miracles, (4) the gift of healing, (5) the gift of tongues, (6) the gift of interpretation of tongues, (7) the gift of discerning spirits." [4] These gifts, then, Walvoord dismisses entirely for the church today for one reason only—*because we don't have them.*

A simple look at the list above clearly shows that only the "miracle" gifts, the signs and wonders, the supernatural ones, are checked off the list. The "permanent gifts" are those which *can* be exercised in the realm of the natural, even in the flesh. They can be fairly well duplicated by education, human effort, assuming authority, or just taking office. So, a man simply starts teaching, and if he has a pleasing personality he is hailed as a "gifted" teacher. If he starts out campaigning with a big tent or rallies in a big hall, with lots of people coming down the aisles, he is known as a "gifted evangelist." If he can raise enough money to undertake his support, he becomes a "missionary." All can be done in the flesh without miracles—no "charisma," no "pneumatikos" about it. Yet this assumes that the role of a teacher is far different from that of one being filled with the Holy Spirit and supernaturally endowed with a gift from God with signs following.

Further evidence of this robbery is found in such words as, "The best explanation of the passing of certain gifts and their manifestation is found in the evident purpose of God in the apostolic age."[5] The terminology "apostolic age" sounds very much akin to the old dispensationalism I was taught some thirty years ago, now labeled "ultra." However, instead of merely dismissing them to a bygone transition period, they now seek to find some temporary purpose for those gifts peculiar to that age to explain their absence today. We seek only to show how a man-made system has robbed us of the possibility of having today what God has intended for us.

At a Bible conference once I heard the words, "Miracles

[4]*Ibid.,* p. 168.

[5]*Ibid.,* p. 173.

are attestation of divine revelation. Revelation has ceased, so, no more miracles." This assumes one basic: that all people everywhere accept the Bible as God's divine revelation. I wish that were true, but the very people we are sent to reach do not accept the Bible as God's Word, and therefore miracles as attestation to the truth are still sorely needed!

Another says, "I boldly assert you never find a child of God healed by faith after the Holy Ghost came into the world on the day of Pentecost." [6] How any intelligent person can make such statements is beyond me. All too many statements in scripture teach "only believe." "If thou canst believe." It was Peter's faith in God that enabled him to say, "In the name of Jesus Christ of Nazareth, rise up and walk" (Acts 3:6). Peter states definitely in verse 16 that "his name, through faith in his name, hath made this man strong."

It is disastrous that just because a man is 2000 years removed from the incident, he can't (or won't) believe it. *To deny miracles today is to deny them in the scripture.* Read Acts 5:16, which took place after Pentecost. And read, "We are his witnesses of these things; and so also is the Holy Ghost whom God hath given to them that obey him" (Acts 5:32). This is exactly the same dispensation we are in today. To witness of these things, as the apostles did, without the witness of the Holy Ghost, is futile.

Robert Anderson writes:

"So also we might expect that the evidential miracles of Pentecost would cease. . . . The purpose of Acts is clear; it bridges the gulf which separates the records of Messiah's earthly ministry to the covenant people, from the apostolic writings addressed to Gentile communities. That book is the history of the Pentecostal dispensation." [7] Of course, Anderson today is labeled as "ultra" by his brother dispensationalists, even though they loudly acclaim the book, *The Coming Prince,* which he wrote later. But, if Acts is history only, why was it included in the canon of scriptures and not treated as were the Books of the Maccabees? Why were the

[6] Alex H. Stewart, *Bodily Healing Since Pentecost* (New York: Loizeaux Brothers), p. 6.

[7] Robert Anderson, *Spirit Manifestations and the Gift of Tongues* (New York: Loizeaux Brothers), p. 23.

miracles set before us like a tantalizing bunch of fruit, if we were only to be told, "Touch not"? How do you explain Acts 2:39, "For the promise is unto you and to your children, and to all that are afar off, even as many as the Lord our God shall call"? These dispensational problems are too big for me to hurdle.

Ryrie writes to his fellow dispensationalists:

"Indeed, the scriptures teach that the Spirit has not given all the gifts to every generation. There were foundation gifts of apostles and prophets (Eph. 2:20), which gifts do not appear in the periods of building the superstructures of the church. Those who were contemporary with Christ experienced certain miraculous gifts of the Spirit which were not experienced by the generation which followed Him (Heb. 2:3-4)."[8]

I would simply ask, "Where does it say that the Spirit has not given all the gifts to every generation?" That one question answered, the whole dispensational system would hold water. But it cannot stand on Ryrie's statement alone. I must find it in my "precious Bible," as George Mueller said.

Prophecy

"This too (prophecy) was a gift limited in its need and use, for it was needed during the writing of the New Testament and its usefulness ceased when the books were completed."[9] If only he could give chapter and verse for this, dispensationalism would stand. But without scriptural precedent it is pure assumption only.

Tongues

"What about tongues today? One cannot say that God would never give this gift or other of the limited gifts today. But everything indicates that the need for this gift has ceased with the production of the written word."[10] We answer simply, "Can the Bible take the place of any work of the Holy Spirit?" One is a very poor substitute for the other. We

[8] Charles C. Ryie, *The Holy Spirit* (Chicago; Moody Press, 1965), p. 84.
[9] *Ibid,* p. 86.
[10] *Ibid,* p. 89.

have yet to find any scriptural precedent for this idea. To state it *as* a fact does not make it a fact.

Discernment of Spirits

"It (discerning of spirits) was a very necessary gift before the word was written, for there were those who claimed to bring revelation from God who were not true prophets." [11] Is Ryrie here trying to say that we do not have such people today? What makes it even worse today and even more deceitful is that these deceivers use the very word of God. They say their teaching is "based on the Bible" even though it may be as false as a green-cheese moon. Indeed, the dispensationalists and their teachings are one of the reasons there is a great need for a resumption of the gift of discernment of spirits.

To say that the canon is complete and therefore there is no longer any need of the miraculous is sheer stupidity. It is true that the Christian needs no signs or authentication. The Bible is his final rule for faith and practice. But the world, the ones we are trying to reach, do not believe the Bible. They do not respect it or know it. Therefore, does not this world still need authentication or "attestation" just as much if not more than it ever did? The very fact that we have the Bible, instead of clarifying the issues, makes it even more confusing to the world because of man's false revelations, false prophets, isms, sects, denominations, and just plain lies from some quarters—all in the name of "the Bible says." *If there ever was a time in the history of the church since Pentecost that needed these gifts, it is now. Today.*

Yet the pamphleteering continues to complete the robbery and eliminate those "damnable Pentecostals" as I have heard several refer to us. "Christians," they say, "should not believe that the Holy Spirit will manifest himself today by the signs of Acts 2:4 any more than they suppose He will manifest Himself today by great physical strength as in the case of Samson." In other words, we are just living in the wrong generation to receive the full strength of God's power and manifestation.

[11]*Ibid*, p. 90.

Is Jesus Christ the same yesterday, today, and forever, or isn't He? Is not the promise still there? The New Testament has not changed. We are still in the dispensation of the Holy Spirit. Samson's strength was not promised to you and me . . . but God's strength was. "He that believeth on me, the works that I do shall he do also; and greater works than these shall he do; because I go unto my Father . . . and I will pray the Father, and he shall give you another Comforter, that he may abide with you forever" (John 14:12, 16).

Another says, "First, we must note that there is no ground in the Word of God for the assumption that the gift of tongues is to be a part of the church experience in the whole New Testament age."

I answer only, "Is there any ground for believing that it won't, other than the fact that you haven't received it personally and therefore think that no one else can?" Acts 2:39 says that the promise of the Holy Spirit will *continue,* and there is no indication that His way of working is any different today:

"The promise is to you [those people standing there listening] and to your children [the next generation] and to all that are afar off [all succeeding generations]." It is as if God knew that some such blighting influence as dispensationalism would come along, and so He added, "even to as many as the Lord our God shall call." There is no "generation gap" here. This sounds to me as if God intended the Pentecostal experience to last.

As part of the great commission, God said, "These signs shall follow them that believe," and there is no parenthesis which adds, "until the Pentecostal dispensation is over." The next change in dispensations is when Jesus comes back to this earth to set up his millennial kingdom. Then these things shall "pass away." Until then, though, the gifts are ours—by faith. If this fact is true, then we are witnessing attempted robbery of the church by dispensationalists.

CHAPTER V

THE OTHER SIDE OF THE FENCE

I am especially partial to R.A. Torrey's emphasis, which is that the baptism of the Holy Spirit is for bringing men to Christ. In his book, *How To Bring Men To Christ,* he devotes an entire chapter to this most important thing. Torrey says:

"There is one condition of success in bringing men to Christ and that is of cardinal importance, and so little understood that it demands a separate chapter. I refer to the Baptism of the Holy Spirit. . . . What is the Baptism of the Holy Spirit? It is a definite and distinct operation of the Holy Spirit of which one may know whether it has been wrought in him or not. . . . The Baptism of the Holy Spirit always imparts power for service, the services to which God calls us. . . . This Baptism is an absolutely essential preparation for Christian work. . . . There must be definite prayer for this baptism. It is often said that the Holy Spirit is already here and that every believer has the Holy Spirit and so we ought not to pray for the Spirit. This argument overlooks the distinction between having the Holy Spirit and having this specific operation of the Holy Spirit. It also contradicts the plain teaching of God's Word that He gives 'the Holy Spirit to them that ask Him.' It is furthermore shown to be fallacious by the fact that the Baptism of the Holy Spirit in the book of Acts was constantly given in connection with and in answer to prayer." [1]

W.S. Boardman, another great stalwart of the faith, adds:

"The first great felt want that arises in the souls is that of deliverance from sin and temptation, met by the grace of God in Christ Jesus. The second great necessity as it arises is that of enduement, power is needed as well . . . enduement

[1] R.A. Torrey, *How to Bring Men to Christ* (Chicago: Revell, 1893), p. 104.

with resurrection life and power in Jesus by the Baptism of the Holy Spirit." [2]

What About Tongues?

Many people ask, "But what about speaking in tongues? What use is it? We don't need tongues anymore."

It would seem some people see no value whatever in gifts which they do not happen to have, whereas all the value is in those gifts which they possess. Regardless of what the scriptures actually say, some still wave aside these "temporary gifts" as of no value, no practical use for either Christian or the unsaved. Briefly, therefore, let us see what God in His Word has to say about just one of His Spirit's gifts, one of the most controversial and talked about—speaking in tongues.

What are tongues for? First I must state that I have never found a serious attempt by any dispensationalist to explain what tongues were for in the early church according to the Bible. If they don't believe it is for today's church, at least they might attempt to show why it was for the early church. But the books say nothing.

The Bible, however, says that the gift of tongues is for several purposes:

1. For personal, private prayer. I Cor. 14:2-4 says that the one who speaks in tongues edifies himself, for he speaks directly to God and not to other men. "Edify" means to "build up" or "improve." How does "speaking in tongues" build or edify? Those who have the gift testify that it is just that, a means of building their faith, enabling them to grow in Christ just as the scriptures promise. They also speak of it as a "release," a big help in their prayer life which is a fulfillment of the prophecy in Isa. 28:11-12, which describes it as a "rest" or "refreshing" even though others might not "hear." Paul's admonitions here seem to clearly imply he was concerned about their abuse of the gift in stated meetings ["when ye come together" (I Cor. 14:26)]. He was bothered by the women's speaking (v. 33-35), the lack of decorum in a service (v. 26-33), neglect of other gifts (v. 22-25), contentment without edification or education (v. 3-22), and possibly

[2] W.S. Boardman, *In the Power of the Spirit.*

other abuses. But in all his "negatives" there are clearly some positives. One of them is that tongues are for personal edification and that the church should never forbid their use.

2. For edifying the church. I Cor. 14 in its entirety leaves no room for mistake. The use of tongues is also for edifying the church, when there is interpretation. Paul wants those who have the gift to "excel" by using the gift to edify the church. The personal gift can, therefore, by development, be nurtured in such a way that that same gift can be used to edify the church. It is clear from I Cor. 14:5 that if an interpreter is present, tongues can be just as edifying as prophecy.

Irving, in the early days of Pentecostalism, emphasized prophecy over tongues, making it the "supreme gift," just as Pentecostals today emphasize tongues as the supreme gift, even to making it the "initial evidence" of the baptism of the Holy Spirit. If practiced in the will and purpose of God, who is to say what gift is better than another? But it is certain that this second use, to edify the church, is a higher, better use of the gift. Paul says, "Seek that ye may excel to the edifying of the church."

3. A sign to the unbeliever. The first two uses of this gift are plainly for the Christian. But just as plainly, God designed a use with the unsaved in mind. The Christian has the gift, but the use is for the unsaved. A "sign" is something "significant." Of what? In every use of the miraculous signs and wonders in scripture, it was a credential, a validation, an attestation. Thus even unbelievers may recognize the presence of God in these gifts. There is no guarantee of this, as verse 21 clearly indicates, but it is another way God in His mercy and love speaks to the unsaved. To our knowledge, this is the only way tongues are used as a "sign," and that is *for the unsaved.*

For a group of Christians to stand around a seeker watching his lips to see if he speaks in tongues, is an abuse of this gift, "wherefore tongues are for a sign, not to them that believe . . . " A Christian who looks for another to speak in tongues as a "sign of the baptism" is biblically out of order. This use of the "sign-gift" needs no interpretation; it would not be understood by the unsaved anyway. But, if someone he *knows* cannot speak his language, his native tongue, rises to bring a message in tongues where he is there in the service, this is significant.

I could take you on such a tour of all nine of the gifts and show you from the New Testament as well as from experience today, that each gift has its use—and its abuse. Each gift has its potential blessing and purpose for the believer and the unbeliever. Used aright, these gifts are for the church today and for the world.

Years ago I accepted the pastorate of a little Baptist church in the state of Maine. This Baptist church and a little Pentecostal church were the only ones in town. The young Pentecostal pastor came to his first church about the same time I came to the Baptist church. I visited him in his home, and we established a friendship. We had joint prayer meetings and street meetings. We swapped pulpits and worked together in many ways. Both churches began to grow in spirit and numbers.

One night my wife and I visited his church unannounced. A very small number of people were assembled. During the song service, the young pastor raised his eyes to heaven and let out a volley of words in some strange language. Although unfamiliar with the practice, I did recognize it as a message in tongues. It was quite lengthy, and soon after came the interpretation. Even as an independent, fundamentalist, separationist Baptist, I had never before felt the witness of the Spirit so strong in my soul. Oh, what strength and encouragement and blessing it was as he prophesied, "God will be with you in your ministry here. Trust in Him. Be not afraid, though there will be those who oppose you . . . "

I sat there, melted in His presence. I just *knew* God was speaking to me. *No dispensationalist can take that away from me, nor can he call it a curse, nor can he say it was Satan, nor can he say I am a Jew.*

While pastoring this same church, I counseled a young wife of only a few months who was having marital difficulties. She came into my study one day in tears. It seems she and her husband could not decide which church to go to regularly.

"I like it here," she began; "the people are wonderful. I was saved in this church. But in my husband's church (Pentecostal) the messages in tongues so often seem just for me, even though I do not speak in tongues myself. They are so helpful, and the people here just don't have these gifts. I guess we just don't believe in them." As her pastor I could do nothing other than advise her to go with her husband. She wanted to go where the demonstration of power was—and I couldn't blame her.

It was at this same pastorate, that I once conducted a funeral in a little country cemetery near West Ripley, Me. One tombstone epitaph read:

> "I came without my own consent,
> Lived a few years, much discontent,
>   At human errors grieving.
> I ruled myself by reasons laws
> But I got contempt and not applause
>   Because of disbelieving.
> For nothing could e'er me convert
> To faith some people did assert
>   Alone would bring salvation.
> But now the grave does me enclose,
> The superstitious will suppose
>   I'm doomed to hell's damnation.
> But as to that they do not know;
> Opinions oft from ignorance flow
>   Devoid of sure foundation.
> 'Tis easy men should be deceived
> When anything's by them believed
>   Without a demonstration."

Some might comment, "Oh, the humanist depravity!" But, I see more! In fact, I hear an honest heart crying for "reality"! If he had only seen a "demonstration" of faith that "some people" only "asserted", he might well have joined Thomas and cried "My Lord and My God!"

CHAPTER VI

THE GIFTS FOR TODAY

One author says, "The Pentecostal gifts of the Spirit recorded in Acts 2:1-4 and Acts 3 are not necessarily for today. Hebrews 2:4 indicates that the gifts involved were evidential for the opening days of the Christian church so that the people who had no written New Testament might have grounds for faith in Christ." After that validation occurred, the sign-gifts were supposedly no longer necessary, and since God never works wonders simply to entertain people, they just vanished.

Quite a philosophy.

Does this author think that just because the canon of scriptures was completed that everyone *had* the scriptures to read and ponder? It was not until around 1500 years *after* Christ that printing was invented. Therefore there were no books, not even the Bible, that anyone could read and study. People did not even know how to read, for there was little purpose in learning to read since there were no books. Only a few scribes had a precious few manuscripts, papyruses or scrolls; nothing existed for the common people. Alas, they still did not have the Word of God, even though the canon was complete at about 100 A.D.

Gutenberg did not come along to change that situation until some 1400 years later. And it was many years after Gutenberg before any significant percentage of the people learned to read. We can safely say that it has been only in the last 300 years that the people have actually "had" the Bible. Can it thus be reasoned that the *written* word was completed, and they no longer needed miracles, signs, and wonders?

Further, we might be surprised to find out how many homes even now do not have a Bible in them. Recently in our city some parents were enraged because their children came home from school bringing Gideon New Testaments. They even wrote letters to the newspaper stating they were incensed at having the Bibles in their homes. Are they any different from people in Jesus' day or the apostolic period? They both are (were) without the Word; both are (were) in need of proof that God is not dead.

The gifts did vanish—they disappeared. But was it because the Bible canon was completed? Or did Christians lose the gifts due to lack of faith, and an emphasis on worldliness and ritual? Was it God's fault or theirs? And then what accounts for the contemporary return of the gifts among people of all denominations as they surrender their wills (and tongues) to the Lord Jesus?

The dispensationalist bases his whole system on this one idea: that the gifts vanished from the experience of the church, therefore they were no longer needed. Yet he never seems to consider why they vanished. Strange, indeed, since all dispensationalists agree that no one should twist his Bible to fit some experience he has had; rather, his experience must be in accord with the Bible teaching. If it's wrong to base one's view of the scripture on their experience, it's wrong to base it on *lack of experience! It isn't right to assume that the reason we don't have these gifts is because we aren't supposed to have them.* I could show where the present-day church doesn't have New Testament love (agape) as Jesus taught it. Does this mean we are not supposed to have love? I know a great many dispensationalists who are possessed by fear and insecurity. Does this mean that Jesus intends for them to live this way? And what about the fact that there is little peace in the world today? Is this because we are not supposed to strive after peace?

Church history clearly records the facts about the waning power of the church. Thomas Payne, in his book, *The Covenant Promise of the Father,* described the whole sad story:

" . . . for as a result of this special baptism of divine power it has by God been decreed, that His Son shall have the heathen for his inheritance, and the uttermost parts of the earth for His possession. . . . Had the early church not degenerated and become worldly, had it not ignored and made sacrifice of this special promise of the Holy Ghost, what mighty inroads would have been made into the Kingdom of Satan. But instead of this special influence of the Holy Spirit being exceedingly prized, and with prayer and self-sacrifice diligently sought and obtained, it soon became with the early church a thing of little or no account. That is, the fiery days of persecution once ended, the former entire dependence upon the upholding power of the Holy Spirit speedily declined, while under our ever increasing degree of worldly mindedness, cumbrous forms and pompous ritual became the things really sought after and esteemed. Thus the Holy Spirit was continually grieved and dishonoured and His powerful influence (as the express promise of the Father) most sinfully sacrificed."[1]

This is the real reason why the Holy Spirit's manifestations vanished. This was "revival in reverse." The very things we need for revival today are the very things the early church gradually lost and relinquished. The supernatural, with the gifts, signs, and wonders, left the church's ministry, indeed, but still man tries to excuse himself from the obvious responsibility, knowing it is all too clear there is now no evidence of power in the church.

But I must speak; I cannot hold my peace with my growing conviction that the answer to today's religious rigidity, formal worship, empty churches, and sterile irrelevancy—is miracle.

John Wesley put it this way:

"It does not appear that these extraordinary gifts of the Holy Ghost were common in the church for more than two or three centuries. We seldom hear of them after that fatal period when the emperor Constantine called himself a Christian . . . from this time they almost totally ceased. . . . The Christians had no more of the Spirit of Christ than the heathens. . . . This was the real cause why the extraordinary gifts of the Holy Ghost were no longer to be found in the Christian church; because the Christians were turned heathen again, and had only a dead form left."[2]

William B. Riley, one of the "fighting fundamentalists,"

---

[1] Thomas Payne, *The Covenant Promise of the Father.*

[2] John Wesley, *Works* (Grand Rapids, Mich.: Zondervan, 1958), 7:26-27.

opposed modernism in his own Baptist schools with a fervor unequaled even in modern times. Concerning the gifts, he wrote:

"That such a tongue existed in the New Testament experience cannot be sanely disproved; that the gifts of the New Testament times were intended for all ages is not the subject of doubt with some of us. With Gordon we affirm that it is impossible for us to look at that rich cluster of promises that hang by a single stem in Mark 16:16-18, and pluck out what suits us, declaring that the rest of them obtained only for a short time. Such treatment of the Word of God is unworthy the sincere students of the Bible. The 'gift' is there, and the 'gift' may be here." [3]

Riley mentioned Gordon. A.J. (Adoniram Judson) Gordon founded the Gordon College of Theology and Missions in Boston, now known as the Gordon-Conwell Theological Seminary. A.J. Gordon says:

"We have maintained in the previous chapter that the Baptism in the Holy Ghost was given once for all on the day of Pentecost, when the Paraclete came in person to make His abode in the church. It does not follow therefore that every believer has received this baptism. God's gift is one thing; our appropriation of that gift is quite another thing. . . . It seems clear from the scriptures that it is still the duty and privilege of believers to receive the Holy Spirit by a conscious, definite act of appropriating faith, just as they received Jesus Christ. . . . There is the same reason for accepting him for his special ministry as for accepting the Lord Jesus for his special ministry. . . . We must withhold our consent from the inconsistent exegesis which would make the water baptism of the apostolic times still rigidly binding, but would relegate the baptism in the Spirit to a bygone dispensation." [4]

(An interesting note: one group of ultradispensationalists have actually done just what Gordon intimates, that is, they have relegated water baptism to a bygone transition period and scrapped the practice rather than accept the truth

---

[3] William B. Riley, *Bible of the Expositor and the Evangelist* (Cleveland, Ohio: Union Gospel Press, 1926).

[4] A.J. Gordon, *The Ministry of the Spirit* (Philadelphia, Pa.: American Baptist Publication Society, 1894), p. 67-68, 72.

that if they accept the command of Jesus to baptize in water they also have to accept his command to be baptized in the Holy Spirit.)

Gordon's emphasis is that one must accept the Spirit for His work, just as they accept Christ for His work for them. Universalism teaches that all men are saved just because Christ died for all men, relieving them of any responsibility to do anything about receiving Christ personally. The dispensationalists, using the same argument, say the same thing about the Christian's relationship with the Holy Spirit, saying that just because the Holy Spirit was given means that automatically all Christians have Him. True, "if any man hath not the Spirit of Christ, he is none of His" (Rom. 8:9). Every Christian is indwelt by the Spirit, but as for receiving the baptism of the Holy Spirit, dispensationalists use the universalist argument to bolster their thesis!

Andrew Murray, a great man of God out of the past, says: "This Baptism of the Spirit is the crown and glory of Jesus' work, that we need it, and must know that we have it, if we are to live the true Christian life. We need it. The Holy Jesus needed it. Christ's loving, obedient disciples needed it. It is something more than the working of the Spirit in regeneration. It is the personal Spirit of Christ making Him present within us, always abiding in the heart in the power of His glorified nature, as He is exalted above every enemy. It is the Spirit of the life of Christ Jesus making us free from the law of sin and death, and bringing us, as a personal experience, into the liberty from sin to which Christ redeemed us, but which to so many regenerate is only a blessing registered on their behalf, but not possessed or enjoyed. It is the enduement with power to fill us with boldness in the presence of every danger, and give the victory over the world and every enemy. . . . To the disciples the Baptism of the Spirit was very distinctly not His first bestowal for regeneration, but the definite communication of the presence in power of their glorified Lord. . . . Just as there was a twofold operation of the one Spirit in the Old and New Testaments, of which the state of the disciples before and after Pentecost was the most striking illustration, so there may be, and in the majority of Christians, is, a corresponding difference of experience. . . . When once the distinct recognition of what the indwelling of the Spirit was meant to bring is brought home to the soul, and [he] is ready to give up all to be made partaker of it, the believer may ask and expect what may be termed a Baptism of the Holy Spirit." [5]

The church today is starving for teaching like that. But we are being robbed just as surely as if they had their hands in the till of our coffers.

Some years ago, in the tabernacle at the Word of Life Camp on Schroon Lake, New York, Charles E. Fuller was the featured speaker. In spite of his dispensational surroundings he electrified the audience with his simple forthright statement declaring that one Sunday shortly before that time, right after going off the air at his Los Angeles radio rally of the Old-Fashioned Revival Hour, someone arose and began speaking in tongues. He motioned for quiet from the rest of the congregation. After the message Charles Fuller said, "Soon, someone arose and gave a beautiful interpretation, a beautiful interpretation." Fuller went on to plead with the people at Word of Life Camp not to be afraid of the Holy Spirit's working.

The Full Gospel Business Men's Fellowship International has published a booklet, compiled by Jerry Jensen, entitled, *Baptists and the Baptism of the Holy Spirit.* The author tells the story of several Baptist preachers, laymen, and laywomen who have come into the charismatic movement and under the power of the Holy Spirit have moved out into extensive ministries. Similar booklets are also available on Methodists, Presbyterians, Episcopalians, etc.

I know of many others, Baptists particularly, who as pastors are bringing their churches into the full light of this renewal. One of them is my good friend, Jamie Buckingham, who is better known to reading America as an author and writer. A Southern Baptist pastor, he is now leading a rapidly growing flock of people from all denominations in a "body ministry" in Melbourne, Florida. His church has broken denominational ties and is growing more rapidly than any other "church" I know of in the state. Occasionally I visit in this open congregation which has no formal membership and

[5] Andrew Murray, *The Spirit of Christ* (New York: Revell, 1888), p. 29, 323.

is composed of hundreds of people from all main-line denominations who have been Spirit-baptized. I see "hippie" looking young people by the hundreds with Bibles under their arms and the sparkle of Christ in their eyes. I see black and white lifting their arms in praise together. I hear the gifts of the spirit in operation—tongues, interpretation, prophecy; and I see healings and miracles take place. It's not unusual at the close of the service (or sometimes at the beginning of the service if the Holy Spirit directs) for the pastor (or whoever else may be leading at that moment) to "give an invitation." Only instead of asking people to close their eyes and bow their heads, the congregation sits alert and expectant as first one and then another rises to his feet and says, "Today I accept Christ as my Savior and make public my belief in Him as my Lord." Statements like this are nearly always followed with great rejoicing on the part of the congregation, praising God, and often spontaneous applause. At other times people will come to the altar or members of the Body will circulate in the congregation, laying on hands and praying for others to be healed or receive the baptism of the Holy Spirit. Yet all things are done decently and in order, and even though these may seem foreign to my background, I thrill to my soul as I feel the Holy Spirit ministering as He did in those early church services in catacombs and upper rooms. The ministry here is vindicated (for those who demand proof in results) by increased ministries (many from this congregation have resigned their jobs and gone to foreign and home mission fields), souls won to Christ, families reunited, and gloom replaced with joy in the believers. Driving back across the state to my home I constantly find myself asking the question, "Why aren't more pastors and Christian workers receiving and using these beautiful gifts of the Spirit?"

Yet I know the reason why. Teaching. Roy L. Laurin says, "Unless at this point we distinguish between the experience of the apostles and the teachings of the apostles, we will be greatly confused. . . . In other words, let us not teach the experience of the apostles in relation to the Holy Spirit, but let us experience the teaching of the apostles."[6]

[6] Roy L. Laurin, *Be Filled with the Spirit* (Los Angeles: American Prophetic League), p. 21.

So, don't teach their experiences, but experience their teachings. Shall we bring the fallacy of this into sharp focus and remind you this means exactly, "Don't do as I do, but do as I say?" The obvious hypocrisy of this is all too obvious to me.

If the apostles' experience is not for us today, why are these experiences recorded for us in the Bible? Just to get us confused? Have you ever stopped to think?—it would have been the simplest thing in the world for God to have left out those portions where miracles were performed. The Holy Spirit could have easily kept Paul from writing I Cor. 14 and Luke from writing those portions of Acts. Without those words there would be no controversy today. If He had wanted us all to be dispensationalists, why did He put Acts 2:39 in the Bible?

I maintain that if healing, tongues, and deliverance are not for us today, then God made a colossal blunder when He allowed those things in the canon of scripture. If He had not told us all about it, I would never have known about it. Perhaps we should just forbid our children to read this section of the Bible since it has no meaning for us today.

A.E. Bishop, way back in 1920, wrote *Tongues, Signs and Visions Not God's Order for Today* with a very commendatory foreword by C.I. Scofield. In Bishop's own introduction he says, "Some of the most renowned Bible teachers of the world have been very kind in answering my questions relating to the miracles and sign-gifts and all are unanimous in believing that the sign-gifts were divinely removed after having accomplished their purposes in the beginning of the present dispensation."[7] With the advent of present charismatic renewal in churches of all denominations, he would have to "pick and choose" his men now.

This underscores our point: The scholars are just the reason why we do not have the gifts as we ought today. Not particularly the men, of course, but what they taught. This devastating doctrine that God divinely removed the gifts has surely continued to rob us.

---

[7] A.E. Bishop, *Tongues, Signs and Visions Not God's Order for Today* (Los Angeles: Biola Book Room, 1920), p. 5.

CHAPTER VII

THE BAPTISM OF THE HOLY SPIRIT

"It was the closing day of the Northfield students' conference, the gathering of the students from the eastern colleges. Mr. Moody (D.L. Moody) asked me to preach on Saturday night and on Sunday morning on the Baptism of the Holy Ghost. On Saturday night I had spoken about 'The Baptism with the Holy Ghost, What it is, What it does, The need of it and the Possibility of it.' On Sunday morning I spoke on 'The Baptism with the Holy Spirit: How to get it.' It was just exactly twelve o'clock when I finished my morning sermon, and I took out my watch and said, 'Mr. Moody has invited us all to go up on the mountain at three o'clock this afternoon to pray for the power of the Holy Spirit. It is three hours to three o'clock. Some of you cannot wait three hours. You do not need to wait. Go to your rooms; go out into the woods; go to your tent; to anywhere you can get alone with God and have this matter out with Him.'

"At three o'clock we all gathered in front of Mr. Moody's mother's house (she was then still living) and then we began to pass down the lane, through the gate up on the mountainside. There were four hundred and fifty six of us in all; I know the number because Paul Moody counted us as we passed through the gate. After a while Mr. Moody said, 'I don't think we need to go any further, let us sit down here.' We sat down on stumps and logs on the ground. Mr. Moody said, 'Have any of you students anything to say?' I think about 75 of them arose, one after another, and said, 'Mr. Moody, I could not wait until three o'clock; I have been alone with God since the morning service, and I believe I have a right to say that I have been baptized with the Holy Spirit.' When these testimonies were over, Mr. Moody said, 'Young men, I cannot see any reason why we should not kneel down right here now and ask God that the Holy Spirit may fall upon us just as definitely as He fell upon the apostles on the day of Pentecost. Let us pray.' And we did pray there on the mountainside. As we had gone up the mountainside heavy clouds had been gathering, and just as we began to pray those clouds broke and the raindrops began to fall through the overhanging pines. But there was another cloud that had been gathering over Northfield for ten days, a cloud big with the mercy and grace and power of God; and as we began to pray, our prayers seemed to pierce the cloud and the Holy Ghost fell upon us. Men and women, that is what we all need—the Baptism with the Holy Ghost." [1]

If I or any other fundamentalist pastor should do anything like this today we would be branded as the worst of fanatics. We would be labeled "holy rollers." Every theological eye within distance would be casting suspicion on our entire ministry. *Yet may God grant the day when once again godly pastors will lead their flocks into this biblical experience, this continuation of the Book of Acts, this personal and church-wide revival so sorely needed.* I would be willing to encounter some wildfire, and deal with it, if only we had the real fire once more.

I find another lesson in the above recounting of this Northfield experience, that is, that every experience must be based on the Word of God. It was after Torrey's two Bible sermons that true results followed. I have visited all too many Pentecostal churches, and most recently too many "charismatic" denominational churches, without hearing any sermons like the one Torrey preached at Northfield. No wonder the fire fell out there in the field; the fuel had already been poured out in the sermon.

How many pastors, next Sunday morning, would have a very much unexpected, unannounced deacons' meeting if they preached on "The Baptism of the Holy Spirit: How to Get It"? But the revival that everybody is talking about and so pitifully few are receiving will come only when men like R.A. Torrey arrive on the scene and start teaching from the

[1] R.A. Torrey, *Why God Used D.L. Moody* (Chicago: Moody Press, 1923), p. 63. Now published by "Sword of the Lord."

Bible exactly what Torrey, Moody, Finney, Gordon, Mueller, Simpson, Murray, and others taught and experienced. Torrey put his finger on it when he said, "Men and women, that is what we all need—the Baptism with the Holy Ghost."

CHAPTER VIII

LET US LOOK AT THE JEW

How does dispensationalism rob us of definite verses of scripture? Remember, one of the chief tenets of the theology of the dispensationalists concerns the distinction between Israel and the church. It is their prerogative, apparently, to pick out the verses that are supposed to be for the Jews, as a nation, and the verses that are for the church. This "pick and choose method" is very convenient, especially when they find something which is out of character for the church today.

Sir Robert Anderson says, "So long, therefore, as the gospel was being proclaimed to the covenant people, miracles abounded. For to the covenant people it was primarily, that Christ came. 'Salvation is of the Jews' the Lord Himself declared . . . " [1] This is dispensationalism, too.

M.R. DeHaan says:

"In this we see (Matthew 10:2-4) the Lord seeks to emphasize that this commission was distinctly apostolic, exclusively for the apostles, for these twelve, and then He commands them saying, 'Go not into the way of the Gentiles, and into any city of the Samaritans enter ye not: but go rather to the lost sheep of the house of Israel' (Matthew 10:5-6). This command of our Lord, then, is explicit and unmistakable, that they are to go with this apostolic message, and with these apostolic gifts only to the nation of Israel, and not to any Gentile whatsoever. It was a strict command: 'Go only to Israel, the kingdom nation.' " [2] But why does he

[1] Robert Anderson, *Spirit Manifestations and the Gift of Tongues* (New York: Loizeaux Brothers), p. 22.

[2] M.R. DeHaan, *Divine Healing and Divine Healers* (Grand Rapids, Mich.: Radio Bible Class), p. 9.

designate the Jews as "the Kingdom nation"?

Here is the fulcrum of this robbery of which we speak. DeHaan goes on to speak of "kingdom signs," "kingdom message," and the "kingdom nation," Israel. Indeed, dispensationalists would have us believe that when the term "this gospel of the kingdom" is used, it is strictly Jewish. At some point (they are disagreed among themselves at just what point) the Jews as a nation were "set aside" and the "parenthesis" started. (Thieme says that tongues was the curse that pinpointed the start of the parenthesis.) Dispensationalism thus teaches that the age we now live in (the church age or "dispensation of grace") will come to an end and God will deal with the Jews as a nation, taking up where He left off. He will supposedly make for them a separate plan of salvation, a different way to be saved than at present. Thus during the tribulation period and on into the millennium the Jews will have a "second chance."

However, such a false theory depreciates the gospel of Christ and God's plan of the ages centered in the cross of Calvary where Jesus Christ died for the sins of the world. *There is now no other way of salvation, and there will never be any other, even for the Jew.* Dispensationalists, however, give the Jew another chance after the rapture.

R.B. Thieme in *Prophecy of Tongues* says, "It is God's will that the Jews are under a curse today." [3] He proceeds to say that as a nation God will not deal with them anymore until the time comes—after their "dispersion." Quoting Isa. 28:11 Thieme says the Jews would be evangelized in the Gentile languages, which he equates with Pentecost. He states that speaking in tongues was for the Jews only and that "the gift of tongues was for the Jews to hear the gospel." However, there is absolutely no scripture to back this up.

The tongues in Acts 2 were not the same as preaching. The only preaching was done by Peter—a Jew. The tongues were only to attract attention—and that they did. Then what? Peter got up and spoke in a language they all understood as Israelites, and then, not before, Peter gave them the gospel message. Thieme completely misses the whole thrust of the

---

[3] R.B. Thieme, *Prophecy of Tongues* (Houston, Texas: Barachiah Church, 1963), p. 3.

meaning of Pentecost to the Jew. It was in their own language they were evangelized after God through signs and wonders (including speaking in tongues) approved the apostle's message which followed. It was because of their speaking in tongues (v. 33) that the dramatic results (v. 41) were accomplished. This is always what tongues are for, never to preach the gospel but only as attestation to the truth.

I have heard more people scoff at "those tongues' people" saying, "If they can speak other languages, why do they have to go to language school like the rest of the missionaries?" This is argued only out of ignorance of what these sign-gifts were given for. *Nowhere will you find that speaking in tongues was given to preach the gospel in someone else's language so that they might be saved.* It is most certainly not exclusively a Jewish gift just because the day of Pentecost was a Jewish feast day and mostly Jews were present. How then would you explain Acts 10 with Cornelius, an Italian?

DeHaan says plainly, "The signs, miracles and wonders Jesus and the apostles performed were also for a definite purpose."[4] Here he couples the miracles of Jesus and the miracles of the apostles together, as being for the same purpose. But herein lies a contradiction: some say the setting aside of Israel took place during Christ's own ministry; others say at Pentecost; even others somewhere about the middle of the Book of Acts; others at the end of the Book of Acts. Some say it "tapered off," always trying to make it coincide with the loss of the gifts from the church.

Remember, then, the line of demarcation between a dispensationalist and a nondispensationalist is that the dispensationalist must keep Israel and the church separate and distinct all the way through. So, these apostolic signs, whether done by Jesus or not, are only for Jews, dispensationalism says. The "system" says that God dealt with the entire world through His chosen people, the Jews, up to a certain point in the New Testament era. To this much we agree. But they go on to maintain, the nation Israel was set aside and the dispensation of the church began, but only as a parenthesis in the overall plan of God's dealing with the nation Israel. This "parenthesis," they teach, is ended at the

---

[4] DeHaan, *op. cit.,* p. 10.

rapture of the church, and once again God will deal with the nation Israel as to their salvation.

As a system this looks good on paper. However, the Bible says God does not have any future plan of salvation for the Jews; it is now or never under the preaching of the gospel in this age or dispensation as promulgated by the church. *No Jew will ever be saved, or anyone else for that matter, outside of the Body of Christ for whom He shed His precious blood, upon which the "second covenant" is based.* This is the reason why God beseeches his people to "leave the camp" of Israel (Heb. 13:12-13) and come to Christ.

The dispensationalists, however, teach that when God takes up again His dealing with the nation Israel (after the rapture of the church) these signs and wonders will in all probability come again. Whenever a new era starts, they maintain, the period is ushered in by signs, wonders, and miracles. (If this be so, then the present outpouring of miracles, signs, and wonders in churches of all denominations indicates the ushering in of the new period—a period which the dispensationalists say has not yet come.) However, a further contradiction is evident, for these same people place a great deal of importance on the "finished Word of God." They say the Bible is the completely revealed will and word of God, that it will never be added to. Yet here they set the Bible aside again for more signs and wonders, which they say were only to validate the preaching of the early church "until the written word of God was completed."

Of course, one does not have to be a dispensationalist to come to these conclusions, for even covenant theologians dismiss the supernatural gifts, all of them at times, by their own "gimmick," saying the new covenant does not cover that period. They, too, have a "transition period" between the covenant times. Therefore, whether a covenant theologian, a dispensationalist, or one adhering to no system, one can conveniently dismiss his own responsibility in this matter by simply arguing that it was God's way of changing the times.

Now, having seen how dispensationalism uses the Jew to invalidate the scripture supporting charismatic claims, let us turn to the church in their system.

CHAPTER IX

THE DISPENSATIONAL CHURCH

Stripped of our credentials, robbed of our potential, and left without the supernatural—what do we have to go by?

DeHaan says:

"The only part of the Bible in existence at the time was the Old Testament. Not a single book of the New Testament had been written. These signs, therefore, were the authentication of the ministry of Jesus and the apostles. These gifts were to approve their ministry as being of God, and were to serve as their credentials while the New Testament was still unwritten. Then when the canon of scripture was completed, and the New Testament was written, there was no more need for these signs and miracles. We are now expected to believe the Gospel, and not to seek for signs and wonders. We are to walk by faith in God's word and not by sight. These signs were for God's miracle nation, primarily . . . "[1]

So, all these miracles of the New Testament, the supernatural happenings of every kind, have been relegated to a bygone transition period and pushed forward to a future dispensation, particularly for Jews and never for the church. Now that dispensationalists have robbed us of our credentials, what do we have in their place to prove that we are preaching the truth?

DeHaan answers:

"We are to be approved of God rightly dividing the Word of Truth. That is the test of the true ministry of the gospel today: rightly dividing the Word, giving to Israel that which belongs to Israel, and to the church that which belongs to the church, and to the world that which belongs to the world."[2]

[1] M.R. DeHaan, *Divine Healing and Divine Healers* (Grand Rapids, Mich.: Radio Bible Class), p. 10.

[2] *Ibid.,* p. 11.

Here you have what appears to me to be the worst conclusion, the direst effects of dispensationalism.

Every sect, ism, and schism proclaims to the housetops, "We have the truth." Yet they contradict each other all the time. I am sure there are sincere Christians among them, believers everywhere who mean to rightly divide the Word of Truth, but I hear dispensationalists all the time who disagree on some mighty important things. Who is right? They do not agree on verses for the Jews and for the church. They disagree over which verses are to be taken literally and which are pictorial. They most certainly disagree on just when the apostolic age was over. Some even deny the miracles recorded in the Bible, explaining them away by natural phenomenon. They just can't agree. So, we ask, how can the effort to "rightly divide the Word" ever replace the credentials, the validation of the truth, which took place in the early church? With all our confusion in the churches today over liberalism and fundamentalism, conservative and neoorthodox, pre-tribulation or post-tribulation, premillennialist and amillennialist, separatist and inclusivist, sinless perfection or holiness, eternal security or conditionalism, Calvinism or Arminianism, predestination or foreknowledge, existentialism, divorce and remarriage, mode of baptism, second coming of Christ (is it at Pentecost, conversion, death, or a visible literal return to earth sometime in the future?)—who are we to believe? Yet all these things are taught under the banner of "the Bible says." Surely we need something to lift us out of the morass and mire of the confusion the church is in, to say nothing of the world which has lost all respect for the church and its irrelevant message of unenlightenment. The church stands today as a tower of Babel (babble) instead of the upper room at Pentecost.

Church history bears out the fact that these signs, wonders, and miracles continued for some 250-300 years after Pentecost. Why? What were they for? Do we need them today?

If I bring a gospel message or testimony to my neighbor he might counter with "But how do I know you are right?"

Shall I say, "Well, you see, I have the truth"? Will that communicate?

"Just show him," the dispensationalist says, "what the Bible has to say."

And I hear my neighbor say, "I don't give a d— what the Bible says." He laughs when I display a Bible. Can my neighbor without Christ, without the Holy Spirit, without any semblance of spiritual perception, rightly divide the word of Truth? Can he discern which of the more than 300 sects, isms, denominations, churches, and religions have the truth? The Bible means nothing to him. How, by rightly dividing it, can he know the truth?

No, the only way I can approach my neighbor is the same way the Holy Spirit approached the unbelievers in the Book of Acts—through signs, wonders, miracles, and, yes, tongues. We need these credentials today. The church needs these attestations of truth today. God's people need the Holy Spirit's witness added to their witness if there is to be successful evangelism in the form of personal soul winning, mass evangelism, missionary work, or any other method of reaching the unsaved for Christ.

Oh, my God, I am so weak and powerless. I am so shallow. I am so needy. I am dry, parched, and empty. Actually, Lord, they have not robbed me. Really, I have just gotten so far away from You and Your intended blessing for me that I have listened to them rather than listening to You. Forgive me, God, forgive me.

> Oh, for a passionate passion for souls,
> Oh, for a fire that burns;
> Oh, for a love that never dies,
> Oh, for a heart that yearns.
> Oh, for a prayer-power that prevails,
> That pours itself out for the lost;
> Victorious power in the conqueror's name—
> Oh, for a Pentecost.

This is the crying need of the church today!

In illustrating, let me show you how dispensationalism has effectively robbed the church and given to the Jew of the past and the future. They take I Cor. 14:21, which is apparently the only verse they see in this chapter, and say, "tongues had the characteristic of being a sign to Israel. Such a sign was necessary at the inauguration of the age of grace to prove to Israel that the gospel message was from God. It had been predicted, 'Nay, but by men of strange lips and another tongue will he speak unto this people' (Isa. 28:11). (This is quoted in I Cor. 14:21-22: 'In the law it is written, by men of strange tongues and by the lips of strangers will I speak unto this people and not even thus will they hear me, saith the Lord. Wherefore tongues are for a sign, not to them that believe, but to the unbelieving.') The fulfillment being fully established, there is no further need for the sign."[3] The same writer states that "this people" can mean only Jews, no Gentiles, not for the church.

Among us fundamentalists there is a commitment to a proven principle of hermeneutics: never take a text out of its context. This is strictly adhered to by the serious, honest Bible student. With this in mind, what is the context of I Cor. 14:21-22? I am sure the honest mind, one uncluttered by biased and preconceived opinions, cannot help but see the context is entirely that of the church. The entire book of I and II Cor. is addressed to the church, and this chapter uses the very word "church" many, many times. It is *for* the church and when "ye come together." Yet these dispensationalists have deliberately plucked out this verse and say that because Isaiah is quoted, it must be that "this people" means and can only mean—Jews. They fail to mention verses 4, 5, 12, 19, and 23 where the word "church" appears. Verse 23 is the very next verse after the phrase, "this people," and any honest exegete will have to maintain that Paul uses Isaiah's quote and applies it to the church.

If this gift were for Jews alone, as a nation of unbelievers, why did Paul, under inspiration, give this to the church? If Paul knew the use of the gifts were to soon die out, all he had to do was keep quiet about it and let the movement die a natural death. His troubles at Corinth would soon be all over, and ours would never be started (ours, that is, on this problem).

[3] John F. Walvoord, *The Holy Spirit* (Wheaton, Ill.: Van Kampen, 1954), p. 186.

Thieme passes over this problem in their system very lightly. "Whether there be tongues, they shall cease," he quotes, and goes on to say, "Corinthians is one of the earlier epistles. Paul never mentions the gift of tongues in some of the later epistles, because the gift of tongues was no longer in use even then. The necessity of its use had already terminated." *This is simply not true.* History bears out these gifts continued for some 300 years after Pentecost. Besides, they have continually cropped up again across the centuries whenever there was a great outpouring of the Holy Spirit—such as today. And Thieme's words still do not explain why Paul wrote about tongues in I Cor. in the first place.

"But," someone counters, "Paul did not know when they would be taken away; this was just a record of what happened to them and was for the Corinthian church only." Maybe Paul didn't know. But the Holy Spirit did. Why did this same Holy Spirit inspire Paul to write these words? If I Cor. 12 and the gifts of the Spirit are not for us today, then this particular portion of the Bible must not be inspired. But if you take out I Cor. 14, then you also have to remove I Cor. 12, for it is here tongues are first introduced as gifts to the church. And if you take out these two chapters, you have to take out the one in between—and that just happens to be I Cor. 13, the best-loved chapter in the entire Bible. It's almost as if God has a sense of humor as he looks upon our "scholarship" and our scissors-wielding "scholars" who try desperately to explain away their powerlessness but cannot do so because God has so arranged these verses in the Bible that they cannot be removed without bringing down the wrath of all Christendom upon them.

Yet men continue to do just that.

And as a result, we are being robbed.

CHAPTER X

LET'S FACE THE WORST

Thus far, the thrust of what I have written has been all in favor of this return to the apostolic, early church distinctions of the Holy Spirit's working, the miraculous, supernatural signs and wonders, the gifts of the Holy Spirit. Are there no words of warning? Is it time for the "all clear" and a signal for "all out" effort with nothing whatever on the other side of the ledger? Are there no dangers and pitfalls?

On the contrary. There are. Indeed, many of the criticisms coming from the dispensational side of the fence are valid and should be faced squarely by every one of us who are in favor of the charismatic renewal.

I would refer you to a book, *The Challenging Counterfeit,* by Raphael Gasson.[1] The author, a former spiritualistic medium, shows how every one of the Holy Spirit's gifts are counterfeited and mimicked by spiritists. From him and many other sources we learn of the tremendous rise of witchcraft, spiritism, and even devil worship. Demonism and other forms of occult religion are seeking to usurp the interests of even Christians who are getting so anxious in the face of the decline of their churches and the modern day labyrinth of sterile denominationalism that they are open to anything that smacks of supernatural power; they see none of it in the church.

In every case that I know anything about, any error in practice by the followers of the "charismatic renewal" is due to false teaching received in the liberal denominations from which they came or to false "guessing" by their critics who themselves do not understand the scriptures, being held in

[1] Raphael Gasson, *The Challenging Counterfeit* (Plainfield, N.J.: Logos, International, 1966).

the anesthesia of dispensationalism. Indeed, the more vocal opponents of this "charisma" teaching are the ardent dispensationalists. I know many independent, nondispensationalist Baptists who are leaning toward divine healing, although still leery about "tongues speaking" or "demon deliverance."

Some of the chief criticism against Pentecostals (and now the charismatic renewalists) is that they do not absorb doctrine (Thieme's words). And I agree that he is probably right. For the most part, Pentecostals have been Arminian in their teaching, some to the extreme of getting saved and lost again, over and over. Some teach sinless perfection even to extremes. This does not characterize the movement as a whole, only certain fringe areas. But what the critics of the charismatic renewal must realize is that coming out of old-line denominations, which have been liberal to the core for many years, these newly Spirit-baptized believers need good, sound Bible teaching on the way of salvation, true holiness, and how to win others to Christ. They will not get this in cold, dead, apostate churches. Therefore they must be taught separation as opposed to compromise and infiltration. Until they come out of those churches and get a solid foundation in a good fundamental, conservative, evangelical church they will continue to do some mighty queer things. Led in the right direction, in Christian love and positive Bible teaching, the movement will go ahead, and I am convinced that this charismatic renewal may be God's last effort to give revival to our churches, a revival which is sorely needed in these last days before His soon return.

CHAPTER XI

MISTAKES

A nutshell study of terminology might help right here. Let's start with two problem terms: "baptism" and "filling." There are some who oversimplify with the statement, "one baptism, many fillings." Very clearly, though, the scriptures teach a "baptism in/of/with the Holy Spirit" which is really the same as becoming filled. The "baptism" is the initial act or experience of entrance into the Spirit-filled life. "Baptism" denotes one precise act at a certain point of time, whereas "filled" with the Spirit denotes the continuing experience of one who has been "baptized" in the Spirit.

In Ephesians, Paul tells his readers, "Be filled with the Spirit" (Eph. 5:18). Here the Greek tense means "go on being filled with" or "continue to be constantly filled." In Acts 4:31 where Luke says they were "all filled with the Holy Ghost," the aorist tense is used, denoting a completed action at a point of time. In this verse the word "baptize" could have been used and mean the same as "filled," but not so in Eph. 5:18 where the concept deals not just with one experience, but with a continuing experience.

Jesus promised, "Ye shall be baptized with the Holy Ghost," and the promise was fulfilled at Pentecost. Yet it reads, "They were all filled," (the aorist again as in Acts 4:31). But when the Word speaks of Stephen, for example, as being "full of the Holy Ghost" (Acts 6:5) that was the continuing presence of the Holy Spirit which began when he was "baptized" in the Holy Spirit. When we realize the root meaning of the word "baptize" (Greek, *baptizo*) is "to immerse," "submerge," and metaphorically, to "overwhelm" or "envelop," we see that what God wants us to know is that at this experience (separate from conversion) we are immersed into His Spirit and then "overwhelmed" by that Spirit.

However, one precaution: in I Cor. 12:13 we have, "For by one Spirit are we all baptized into one body," and here the preposition is "by" not "in," "of," or "with." So, do not confuse this act of the Holy Spirit which places us into the Body of Christ with the experience we speak of here.

The reference in I Cor. 12:13 is to the "one baptism" that saves as in Eph. 4:5. We cannot deny that there are at least three baptisms taught in the scripture. They are: water baptism, baptism in the Holy Spirit, and baptism into the Body of Christ. We can baptize people in water. The Holy Spirit baptizes us into the Body of Christ, and Jesus baptizes us in the Holy Spirit. Each case is a distinct experience. The baptism into the Body of Christ is the entrance into the family, the true church, which is conversion. This has to do with our "standing" or "position" in Christ. This is not the empowering for service in which Jesus places the Spirit into us. John said, "He [meaning Jesus] shall baptize you with the Holy Ghost and with fire."

It can be illustrated this way: a glass is placed into a pail of water (baptized, submerged, immersed). The empty glass immediately "fills" with water and is full. So with us. First we are placed into the Spirit, then the Spirit is placed into us. However, a closed glass can be in the Spirit, but will never receive the Spirit until it opens itself to that which is all around.

Just as "filled with" or "full of" is the continuing growth of the "baptism in the Spirit," so salvation is the continuing growth of conversion. Conversion is a once-for-all act or experience at a certain point of time. It's improper to speak of a "converted person" without reference to the conversion experience. Salvation, however, refers to a period of time, not a point in time. The Greek language is beautiful in this respect in that it clears all this up for us by adding another tense to our simple past, present, and future. It is called the aorist. This tense denotes a completed action, not something that started in the past and continues. For instance, "saved" would be aorist, and "salvation" would refer to the simple present tense. Christians *were* saved (Matt. 1:21; 18:11;

I Tim. 1:15; I Cor. 1:21). Christians *are* being saved (Rom. 8:24; I Cor. 1:18; Rev. 21:24). And Christians *will be* saved (Heb. 7:25; Matt. 10:22; Acts 15:11). Salvation, then, is the continuing experience of conversion, such as Paul speaks of when he says, "work out your own salvation with fear and trembling" (Phil. 2:12). So, the "filling" is the continuing experience of the baptism of the Holy Spirit.

[The word "baptism" is not a translation of a Greek word into English. Rather it is a transliteration of the Greek word *"baptizo"* meaning to dip, submerge, or immerse. The word is used in many other ways other than in reference to Spirit or water baptism. Tailors who dyed clothes "baptized" them into their vats. When the seventy commissioned by King James to translate the Bible into English arrived at this word they decided to create a new word, baptize, rather than to give an accurate translation (immerse) since it went contrary to their theology. The entire seventy believed only in sprinkling or pouring for water baptism. They couldn't accurately translate the word and still maintain their standing with the Church of England. However, Thayer, author of the Greek-English lexicon, even though a Unitarian, honestly (against his theology) asserts that "immerse and submerge or dip" is the literal meaning.]

Terminology loses some of its significance when we realize that the six experiences of the "baptism" in Acts were definitely charismatic extensions of Pentecost. The experiences are recorded as: "filled" (Acts 2:4), "filled" (Acts 4:31), "fallen upon" (Acts 8:16), "received" (Acts 8:17), "filled" (Acts 9:17), "fell on" (Acts 10:44), "poured out" (Acts 10:45). Of this latter experience, Peter testifies that these Gentiles had "received the Holy Ghost as well as we." Those last four words identify it as the same experience Peter had at Pentecost. Acts 11:17 further states, "God gave them the like gift as he did unto us." In Acts 19:6, we read that the Ephesians came into their Pentecost as "the Holy Ghost came on them."

These experiences cover about twenty years, yet are all linked together as fulfillment of Jesus' promise, "Ye shall be *baptized* with the Holy Ghost." Thus these various terms all mean the same thing. So, despite the problems we have with terminology, the experience itself outweighs any value of our intelligence to perceive just the correct terms for it.

In 1956 while pastoring in Maine, I was publishing a paper entitled *Revival Fires*. I wrote the following commentary: "It is interesting to note that no one in Moody's day dared dispute his experience or his terminology. They couldn't because of the unmistakable results or evidence of his ministry. Many today try to cover up by saying, 'Well, Moody was not a great scholar; he had very little education; intellectually, Moody was quite ignorant; thus, he did not have the right terminology, and what he had was simply an experience of . . . ' *Many people are intellectual enough to explain his experience away, but personally, I'd rather have Moody's experience than their intellectualism."* [1]

C.I. Scofield probably has done more than any other man since John Darby to popularize the dispensational system. Dr. John R. Rice, in his excellent booklet, *How Great Soul Winners Were Filled with the Spirit,* says:

"That Moody's work was done in the mighty power of the Holy Spirit, that he really had upon him the power of Pentecost, was obvious to all who knew him well. At Moody's funeral, C.I. Scofield, then about 56 years old, spoke. And though later when there was such a hue and cry raised by the followers of Darby against the terminology of Moody and Torrey and other great soul winners on this matter of the Baptism of the Holy Spirit, or the fulness of the Spirit, Scofield avoided it, yet on this occasion he used the terminology of Moody and of Torrey and Finney. Here are Dr. Scofield's words over the body of the great soul winner, Moody. 'The secrets of Dwight L. Moody's power were: First in a definite experience of Christ's saving grace. He had passed out of death into life, and he knew it. Secondly, he believed in the divine authority of the Scriptures. The Bible was to him the voice of God and he made it resound as such in the conscience of men. Thirdly, he was Baptized with the Holy Spirit, and he knew it. It was to him as definite an experience as his conversion.' *(The Life of D.L. Moody,* by his son, page 561)."[2]

[1] *Revival Fires,* Harmony, Maine, 1956.

[2] John R. Rice, *How Great Soul Winners Were Filled with the Spirit* (Wheaton, Ill.: Sword of the Lord Pub., 1949), p. 6.

It was this driving passion of D.L. Moody's to win souls that caused him to long to see all his workers believing and experiencing what he had. He went to great lengths to get those under him to believe in and receive the baptism with the Holy Spirit.

Initial Evidence

A very natural question arises in the inquiring mind of anyone encountering this line of teaching: "How can one know when he becomes filled with the Holy Spirit?" This is a normal question, just as one when first approached about "being saved" asks, "How do you know when you are saved?"

Some emphatically state that speaking in tongues is the initial evidence of the baptism in the Holy Spirit. This is the acknowledged position of such groups as the Assemblies of God. Others just as loudly proclaim that the greatest evidence of the work of the Spirit in anyone's life is the fruit of the Spirit.

To their credit, the Pentecostal believers have tried to communicate to the inquiring mind which asks, "How can I know?" They are unashamed of their position and have written profusely along these lines. But how many books have you read by fundamentalists on the subject?

Dispensationalists and charismatic theologians are agreed that there is no better, more Biblical or practical way to know that you *are* filled than by the fruits of the Spirit through your life. The Bible makes that clear in Eph. 5 and even more specifically in Gal 5:22-23. This matter is not up for question here; but what *is* up for question is: "How can I know when I first become filled (baptized) with the Spirit?"

The dispensationalists who answer, "By their fruits ye shall know them," are not meeting the question fairly, mostly because they confuse the matter of the "baptism" with the continual "filling." Many theologians believe in being "filled with the Spirit" (at least they use that terminology) but they completely sidestep that initial experience of receiving it, which is the baptism of the Holy Spirit. Some explain, "We all got it back on the day of Pentecost. That's the only baptism in the Spirit there is." They look on it as 2000-year-old representative experience never to be received by contemporary Christians. Herein lies the "confusion of tongues" today, one group elevating it to the stature of being "the initial evidence" while another relegates the whole thing to a bygone transition period. One fulfills prophecy with it today; the other calls it a fulfilled prophecy of yesterday.

This confusion was pointed out again to me recently when a man, brand new in the charismatic movement, talked with me in my office. He had recently left his charismatically oriented Baptist church because, as he stated it, "I just cannot understand this tongues' business." His father had been a minister in a staid, old-line denominational church. Now the son was finding it difficult to orient himself. He was much confused over the teaching that tongues was the "initial evidence" (which was what that particular church taught). He felt he was being pressured into "tongues speaking."

I explained: "God will give you the gift He wants you to have in His own time, and the Bible evidence you are seeking. Just believe in the experience you have and worship God. Don't doubt. Serve Christ. Witness for Him, and fellowship where you can be fed. Do not despise tongues nor those who use them. Ask for all the gifts and allow the Holy Spirit to give you those which He desires."

The mind should be centered on the Baptizer and not the baptism, the Giver and not the gift. The strict emphasis should be on seeking the Lord and His blessing, whatever that specific experience might be; not a certain gift, whatever that gift may be. The "desire" Paul speaks of in I Cor. 14:1, the "zeal" (14:12), and the "coveting earnestly" (I Cor. 12:31), come *after* (or at the same time) but surely do not refer only to one certain gift.

Dispensationalists downgrade, laboriously and painstakingly pamphleteer against, and even ridicule any seeking after the "gifts of the Spirit." They say that this "seeking" produces schizophrenia, maniacal tendencies, psychoses, mental aberrations, and hallucinations. It is true. False teaching does do this. But I have seen dispensationalists in jail; does that prove anything? Only that the fundamental gospel they preach just didn't sink in. Yet when a "holy roller" gets in trouble, some immediately pounce on this as a point against Pentecostal teaching of the baptism of the Holy Spirit and "those tongues' people."

This is downright unfair. People are already crazy (or headed in that direction), and they seek after the gifts because in them they sense the possibility of regaining their normalcy. Men don't go crazy seeking God's gifts. They seek God's gifts because they are going crazy. There is quite a difference.

Therefore, even though I do not believe that tongues is the initial evidence (or should I say not *always* the initial evidence), the Bible is still the final authority. I must state that without the strong stand by Pentecostals, without the fellowship I enjoyed in their midst, I would not now have the basic understanding I do about these things (in spite of the fact that I have seen and rebelled against some of their teachings, excesses, and extremes). Without their ministry to me, however, I would still be floundering in denominational dispensationalism (or dispensational denominationalism)! I am eternally grateful for all I received.

CHAPTER XII

REAL EVIDENCE

In every case in the Book of Acts where groups or individuals were filled with the Spirit, there was some outward evidence. Let's study that premise:

1. *Acts 2:1-13.* Reading carefully we see evidence of the Spirit's work on the 120 believers at Pentecost. The evidences were a rushing mighty wind, cloven tongues like as of fire, and speaking with other tongues. These were three definite signs or significant manifestations of the Spirit whereby the early church knew that Christ's promise was being fulfilled in them. Included in this group who spoke in tongues was Mary the mother of Jesus.

2. *Acts 4:31.* This verse tells us, "they were all filled with the Holy Ghost," and then there were two outward manifestations: the place was shaken where they were assembled and they all spoke the Word with boldness. These, by the way, were the same ones who just days before had received their initial baptism at Pentecost.

3. *Acts 8:5-19.* Verse 17 says, "and they received the Holy Ghost." It is clear from the context that this was not their salvation, for verse 12 says that before this "they believed Philip" who had "preached Christ unto them." Verses 6-8 give many evidences of their salvation. The evangelists, though, realizing a lack, asked for help from the home church which "sent unto them Peter and John: who when they were come down, prayed for them. that they might receive the Holy Ghost; (for as yet he was fallen upon none of them, only they were baptized in the name of the Lord Jesus.) Then they laid their hands on them and they received the Holy Ghost." This happened after salvation and was accompanied by the laying on of the hands of the apostles.

A person must receive the person of the Holy Spirit as a matter of definite experience, just as one receives the person of Christ at conversion. What was the evidence? We don't know. The scriptures do not say. But *Simon saw something* (or heard something). Unsaved himself, or at least undiscerning (it does say that he also believed, so he may have been a Christian), he discerned some external evidence to let him know that something had taken place in the lives of these others—and whatever it was, he wanted the same power to administer it to others. We cannot deny that this may have been speaking in tongues since that was the most common evidence.

4. *Acts 9:9-18.* This is Paul's experience, apparently when he was alone with Ananias. Verse 17 says Paul (Saul) was "filled with the Holy Ghost" three days after his conversion on the road to Damascus. Verse 18 gives the outward evidence: "Immediately there fell from his eyes as it had been scales; and he received his sight forthwith." Healing. then, was Saul's initial evidence of his baptism. Of course, Paul did speak in tongues. On his own admission he said, "I thank my God I speak with tongues more than ye all" (I Cor. 14:18). But there is no evidence that Paul spoke in tongues when he was filled with the Spirit—although we cannot deny he may have since he later equates his experience with the one the other apostles received at Pentecost.

5. *Acts 10:44-46.* The "gift of the Holy Ghost" was "poured out" on the Gentiles. This is different terminology, but it was the same experience. That it was the "baptism of the Spirit" is verified by the terms or phrases in verse 45: " . . . also was poured out the gift of the Holy Ghost." Notice that word "also," indicating it was on the Gentiles as well. This plainly refers the reader back to the Jewish friends of Peter's who had received this same experience at Pentecost. Recounting this experience in Acts 11, Peter says, " . . . the Holy Ghost fell on them, as on us at the beginning" (v. 15), and, " . . . God gave them the like gift as he did unto us" (v. 17). Surely, then, this was the same baptism in the Spirit which was received at Pentecost. What outward evidence came there? Acts 10:46 says that those who came with Peter, the Jews, knew that these Italians were filled with the Spirit

for "they heard them speak with tongues and magnify God." Peter and those who came with him who had received their baptism on the day of Pentecost knew that Cornelius' household was receiving the same thing because they heard them speak with tongues. Speaking in tongues, then, surely here is the outward evidence. No amount of hermeneutical chicanery by dispensationalists or anyone else can explain this any other way, although some try by saying this was the "Gentiles' Pentecost," seeing the Jews had theirs on their day some years before.

6. *Acts 19:1-6.* This takes place twenty years after Pentecost. The Ephesians, soon to become the most highly spiritual church in New Testament times, had been saved under Apollos' ministry. That they were Christians is evidenced by Paul's question: "Have ye received the Holy Ghost since ye believed?" or as the ASV more correctly renders the original Greek, "Did you receive the Holy Ghost when ye believed?" Paul would not have asked such a question if they were not already saved. Rather, Paul, soul winner and spiritual diagnostician that he was, would have asked them, "Have you received Jesus Christ as your personal savior?"

Some would have us believe that these people were simply converts of John the Baptist (knowing only the baptism of repentance). But in Acts 18:24 we are told that Apollos was the one who took the gospel to Ephesus. What did Apollos teach? John's water baptism only? No! Again from the ASV we read that Apollos "spake and taught accurately the things concerning Jesus" (Acts 18:25). Thus the Ephesians had the true gospel, the gospel of Christ.

But Apollos was lacking something, for we read in that same verse that he preached "knowing only the baptism of John," which is the baptism of repentance of sin. He did not know the baptism of the Holy Spirit. Paul, arriving on the scene as recorded in Acts 19, saw their lack and changed the situation. They had not even been water-baptized properly. He took care of that, and then Paul laid hands upon them, the Holy Ghost came on them, and they spake with tongues and prophesied. Here then the evidence is twofold: tongues and prophecy.

We have looked at six experiences in the Book of Acts

where people were filled with the Holy Spirit. We have seen nine definite charismatic "initial evidences": (1) rushing mighty wind, (2) cloven tongues like as of fire, (3) speaking with other tongues, (4) the place was shaken, (5) they spoke the word with boldness, (6) speaking with other tongues again, (7) divine healing, (8) speaking with tongues again, and (9) prophesying. No Bible student can deny this. This is a realistic deduction of actual scriptures taken well within the context or framework of this subject. Although I personally feel that one of these is just as much an "initial evidence" as any one of the others, I must hasten to point out that speaking in tongues *is* mentioned three times out of the nine, making it the most common evidence. Thus to be scriptural, one must conclude that most people will speak in tongues when they are "filled with the Spirit." Most "seekers" are not satisfied until they have had the experience of speaking in tongues. Man-made, convenient systems which excuse us from the plain weight of evidence are not sufficient when weighed against the plain Word of God.

In the New Testament there are many references to the "filling" or "baptism" of the Holy Spirit. Dr. C.I. Scofield cross-references these verses in his *Scofield Reference Bible,* and in almost every case when the filling or baptism of the spirit is mentioned, he refers his readers back to Acts 2:4, "and they were all filled with the Holy Ghost and began to speak with other tongues, as the Spirit gave them utterance." Thus even the chief dispensationalists cannot deny that the filling of the Holy Spirit was nearly always accompanied by the speaking in tongues. Despite all his teachings to the contrary, when it came to the Word of God this scholar was forced to recognize that the most common evidence of the baptism of the Holy Spirit was speaking in tongues, as in the Pentecostal experience. Perhaps the most interesting cross-reference made by Dr. Scofield is the one on John 7:38-39: "He that believeth on me, as the Scripture hath said, out of his belly shall flow rivers of living water. (But this spake he of the Spirit, which they that believe on him should receive: for the Holy Ghost was not yet given; because that Jesus was not yet glorified.)" And in the margin of the *Scofield Reference Bible,* in reference to these words of Jesus, is "Acts 2:4" again. (It is significant that most who receive the gift of tongues testify that it starts deep inside their being and flows out to the tongue.)

Is it unreasonable to want evidence? All who believe the Bible and teach conversion as an experience also teach that a person may know he is saved because the word clearly states, "His Spirit bears witness with our spirit that we are the children of God" (Rom. 8:16). This is an inner evidence which may take on any aspect from joy to peace. The Lord allows this inner witness as an evidence (although it will later take on outward aspects also). However, with the baptism of the Holy Spirit this is not so. Without exception the scriptures always record some outward evidence as an initial sign of the baptism. And those who deny such signs are denying the scriptures.

This raises the problem of the effective ministry of many who do not believe in this work of the Spirit. That there are many, greatly used of God, who don't teach this experience, is quickly agreed. Any true Christian, born by the Spirit into the family of God on simple childlike faith, who yields himself to God and His Spirit, may be used of God in winning souls. But although a person may be used of God to win souls, if he is caught up in dispensational dogma, he will never be able to pass on the benefits of his own blessings. His converts will be like drones in a beehive, useless unless they somehow get the message of the secret to His power. That secret is the baptism of the Holy Spirit. Conceivably, they could be filled or baptized in the Spirit and not know it, because they are so ignorant of charismatic truth. However, just as it is conceivable that a person could be saved and not know it, such occurrences are rare. However, I do believe that many Christians have been baptized in the Holy Spirit, but because of dispensational errors have never appropriated the wonderful gifts of the Spirit as promised in I Cor. 12 and Acts 2:39. Once they shake off the bondage of dispensationalism and become open to the simple meaning of the Word of God, it is often with joy and thanksgiving that they reach out and claim through immediate use the gifts of the Spirit—tongues included.

The real reason I believe this is that so many men are

"better than their creed." I don't really believe they believe what they say they believe. Sooner or later, these men will come to the same position as the charismatic ministries teach, realizing that all the gifts are given to edify the church and equip the man of God for the ministry of winning souls. This, by the way, is the evidence that Jesus listed for those who had received the power of the Holy Ghost. "Ye shall receive power, after that the Holy Ghost is come upon you, and you shall be witnesses unto me . . . " (Acts 1:8). Jesus says it was for this purpose that the Holy Ghost was sent, and Paul indicates that the gifts are but tools to help with the ministry of soul winning.

I recall the story of an old farmer who died, leaving his huge farm to his son. Although the farmer had always plowed the fields with a mule and hand plow, just before he died he had paid cash for a new tractor and plow. When it came time to plant, the son hitched up the mule and started out, one row at a time, turning over the ground to receive the seed. His neighbor, knowing the tractor was in the shed, encouraged the son to use the new tools. The son, however, was a stubborn dispensationalist and refuse to use the new tools. The result was that although he had a good crop, the neighbor's crop was ten times the amount of his, simply because the neighbor used the powerful equipment.

The gifts are tools. They are not meant to be exhibited ("Look, I have the finest hoe!") but are meant to be used. And, if I might add a note, they are meant to be used to bring forth fruit which IS to be exhibited (for by their fruit—not their gifts—shall ye know them).

People who have the Word of God without the Spirit
    Dry up.
People who have the Spirit without the Word
    Blow up.
Those who have the Word and the Spirit,
    Grow up.
And when Jesus comes, will
    Go up!

CHAPTER XIII

RESULTS

All Bible scholars, dispensationalists included, are agreed there is no greater proof of the Holy Spirit's ministry in a life than the fruits of the Spirit. These fruits are the result of the indwelling Spirit, received at conversion. However, it's only when a person is filled with the Spirit that these fruit begin to be produced in abundance. Like the gifts, there are nine of them, and they are listed in Gal. 5:22-23: love, joy, peace, long-suffering, gentleness, goodness, meekness, faith, and temperance.

There is no real fulfillment in the Christian life until these fruits are manifested. But let me warn you, you'll go crazy trying to "put on the fruits" without having cultivated them with the gifts and having them brought to natural maturity through the Spirit. Trying in the flesh brings only misery. Try to "put on love" and you'll find it only a put-on. Try feigning joy, and everyone, including yourself, will recognize the facade. You do not fool even yourself when you try to have peace. The only answer is the fullness of the Spirit.

Charles G. Finney, former attorney and later one of the world's most famous evangelists, relates his experience with supernatural joy and love when he tells how it was manifested in his life at the baptism of the Holy Spirit.

"As I closed the door and looked around, my heart seemed liquid within me—there was no fire in the room nor any light, nevertheless it appeared to me to be perfectly light. As I went in and shut the door, it seemed as if I met the Lord Jesus face to face. He looked down at me in such a manner as to break me right down to His feet. . . . I must have continued in this state for quite some time; but my mind was too absorbed in the interview to recollect anything I said. As soon as my mind remained calm enough to break off the interview, I returned to the front office and found that the fire I had made of large wood was mostly burned out. But as I turned and was about to take a seat by the fire, I received a mighty baptism of the Holy Ghost. I could feel the impression like a wave of electricity going through me and through me. Indeed it seemed to come in waves and waves of liquid love; for I couldn't express it any other way. He (the office boy) found me in this state of mind and said unto me, 'Mr. Finney, what ails you?' I could make no answer for some time; then he said, 'Are you all right? Are you in pain?' I gathered myself up as best I could and replied, 'No, but I'm so happy I-I-I can't live!' " And the next day after that restless night "I arose upon my knees in bed and wept aloud with joy, and remained for sometime, too much overwhelmed with the Baptism of the Spirit to do anything but pour out my soul to God. . . . These waves continued to roll over me and over until I recollect I cried out, 'I shall die if these waves continue to pass over me!' I said, 'Lord, I cannot bear anymore!' Yet I had no fear of death. How long I continued in this state with this baptism continuing to roll over me and go through me I do not know." [1]

Soul Winning

Evangelism is the primary task of the church, and all spiritual growth and blessing from God is for this purpose. There is only one way, through Christ. "I am the way, the truth and the life," Jesus said. That "way" is straight and narrow while the wrong way is wide "and many there be that go in thereat" (Matt. 7:14). This is fundamental and this is why I am a "fundamentalist."

Just this week I had a lady tell me, "I believe all the churches are trying to do the same thing. They are all serving Christ." I may have offended her slightly when I abruptly answered, "I could really say I wish that were so, but some churches are working for the exact opposite. They most certainly are not serving Christ." I cling to the fundamental belief that Christ is the only way and so I am a fundamentalist.

[1] Charles G. Finney, *Autobiography* (Chicago: Revell, 1903).

We are urged by the Bible to be "fishers of men." And, God hasn't left us without bait, hooks, poles, lines, and nets for the job. He has thoroughly equipped His Church. Yet most churches go fishing for lost souls and leave their equipment (the gifts) home in the closet, or even worse, deny that they even exist. If souls are like "fish," and we are the "fishermen," then we need a pole which supports the line, hook, and bait. This is the Word of God. We need a "line" which is our testimony and the gospel of Christ. To this line is tied a "hook," and this hook is the particular way the gospel is applied. It could be an "invitation," a challenge in a public service to get up and tell what the Lord has done for them, or personal evangelism. Something has to be done to get them to DO something about it. One of the most necessary parts of a fisherman's rig is the bait. This has to entice the "fish." The bait lures them, the hook secures them, the line wins them, and the pole brings them in. But what is the bait? The gifts and the fruits of the Spirit.

If miracles in the New Testament were for attestation, approbation, and confirmation ("confirming the Word with signs following"), is there any valid reason why we cannot ask and expect God to confirm His Word today? *These gifts the miracles, signs, and wonders, would do more to "lure" the sinner to God, entice the unbelieving to faith, attract the wary and skeptical to the solid rock of Christ, than any Sunday school promotional campaign, revival gimmicks, every-member canvass programs or pack-the-pew plan I know.* The gifts "worked" in Jesus' day and still do today when Spirit-filled men and women are willing to be channels for their working. I am convinced that many people are just waiting for more "evidence," more downright honest-to-goodness "reality" in the Christians and their words and works.

One of the basic rules in writing is "show, don't tell." Signs and wonders show forth the power of God. And significantly, it was a particular sign (tongues) that "lured" the fish to the Big Fisherman at Pentecost and resulted in the greatest revival in history—all without the benefit of newspaper ads, gold stars for attendance, or Madison Avenue Techniques. In fact, those early apostles didn't even have a bus ministry—all they had was the power of God upon them.

Thus God expects us to use and appropriate both the gifts and the fruit of the Spirit. To refresh your memory, let me list the two side by side.

GIFTS:	FRUIT:
word of wisdom	love
word of knowledge	joy
faith	peace
healing	patience
miracles	gentleness
prophecy	goodness
discerning of spirits	faith
tongues	meekness
interpretation of tongues	self-control

We cannot compare or arbitarily contrast these two fields of "equipment" God has left His church. He expects us to exhibit both. Indeed, one set of "gifts" or "fruit" will complement the other set of "fruit" or "gifts." Let me illustrate.

We will win souls to Christ through love (Rom. 5:5). By showing the real joy of the Lord in our countenance, our words, and our acts, we will win more to Christ than by all the miracles we could perform without joy. The signs, gifts, and wonders were only to attest to the truth that followed: preaching, testimony, song, and prophecy. At Pentecost, the dispersed Jews coming from all those foreign lands for the feast day were "amazed," "confounded," and "marveled" asking, "What meaneth this?" This was just what Peter was waiting for. He then preached, and through his preaching the Jews were convicted by the Holy Spirit and asked, "What shall we do?" Peter told them exactly, and some 3,000 were won to Christ. *This is always the result of a biblical Pentecostal experience.* The baptism of the Holy Spirit was given explicitly so the believer could be empowered to win others to Christ.

Healings may abound, but without the fruit and the simple gospel message they are ineffective. Devils may be cast out, but unless the fruit of the Spirit is instilled it avails nothing. These "display miracles," as some theologians have come to call them, are for the unsaved, to be sure, but are only to start their thinking, attract their attention. As in the early church, they are to be our credentials, showing the approval of God upon our ministry and letting others know we are telling the truth. Miracles, signs, and wonders win no one to Christ. They must also hear the gospel. But the gifts of the Spirit are given to whet the appetite of the unbeliever so they will "hunger and thirst" after righteousness until they, too, are filled.

Objections

I constantly hear people say, "Yes, I want to be filled with the Spirit, but I don't want anything to do with tongues." My friend, you can't bargain with God. This may be the very thing He would have you to do in order to prove Himself to you. It will become your initial evidence. Of course, if you mean it when you tell God you want nothing to do with tongues, He will honor your request. But you will be the loser, for unless you accept all God has for you, you will miss out on receiving the "fullness" of the Spirit. You will be like a glass with a rock in the bottom. It can be filled, but as long as the rock is in the bottom it is not completely full—for the rock (your rebellion against God) still occupies a place that God's Spirit longs to take over. God will not give a gift, however, to anyone who does not want it. A gift at the foot of a Christmas tree must be taken—as well as given.

"Lord, I want to be filled, but all this emotionalism is too much. I just can't stand it." Dear soul, He may lead you through to the place of "magnifying God" like those Italians did in Acts. It may come to you so powerfully that people will wonder about you. They called Peter and the others at Pentecost drunk. You may be due for the greatest emotional upset you ever had. On the other hand, those nearby might not even know anything is going on, you are so undemonstrative. Just don't dictate to God how He should fill you, for He cannot and will not be put into a mold.

Someone else says that tongues are divisive. "I've never known a church yet that wasn't split in two when those tongues' people got going." Let me say this about that matter. Tongues (and healing and miracles and signs and wonders) are of Jesus. And Jesus is divisive. Let Jesus Christ walk into any church in America today and He will divide that congregation into those for Him and those against Him. The things of God are always divisive, for they make people come to a point of total yieldedness. And as long as there are those with stiff necks and hard hearts who rebel against the guidance of the Holy Spirit, there will be divisions. But it's not the "tongues' people" who cause the rebellion, but those who are resisting the power of the Holy Spirit. When that former cripple came walking and leaping and praising God into the Temple, he caused division. Miracles always do this. But they also draw crowds, and Peter took the occasion to preach to the crowd about Jesus Christ. And as a result was put in jail for it. The Word of God is a two-edged sword, and the Holy Spirit, working through his people, will "rightly divide the word of truth." Tongues did not divide at Pentecost. Why? *Because they were all together in one accord.* Jesus had told them to wait, and as they waited in expectancy they were willing to take anything He gave them. And when the people of God, today, become willing to take anything God gives them (including tongues) there will be no divisions.

God, however, does not always work in the same way. Contrast the tremendous emotional upheavals in the lives of men such as Moody and Finney to the deep experience of George Mueller. Andrew Murray writes in his book, *The Two Covenants,* of Mueller:

"In the life of George Mueller of Bristol there was an epoch four years after his conversion to which he ever after looked back and of which he often refers as his entrance into the true Christian life. Mueller says, 'God, God became my portion. I found my all in Him; I wanted nothing else. And by the grace of God this has remained, and has made me an extremely happy man, and it led me to care only about the things of God. . . . It was my beginning to understand this point in particular which had a great effect upon me; for the Lord enabled me to put it to the test of experience by laying aside commentaries and almost every other book and simply reading the Word of God and studying it. The result of this was that the first evening that I shut myself into my room to give myself to prayer and meditation over the Scriptures, I learned more in a few hours than I had done during a period of several months previously. But the particular difference was that I received real strength in my soul in doing so. . . . The office of the Holy Spirit I had not experimentally understood before that time.' "[2]

But is this experience for just "great men"? Is it not for all? I will never forget a nine-year-old girl sitting on the front seat of a church, drinking in the message from God's Word, sitting quietly with her arms folded. Soon I noticed her eyes closed, and then a beautiful smile spread over her face, one of sheer joy and ecstasy. With her arms still folded throughout the entire experience, with no audible sounds which I could hear (although her lips were moving rapidly), and with sometimes a little toss of her pretty hair as her face was uplifted to God, He filled her with His blessed Spirit. Unemotional, quiet, still—but the work of God was being done. Later, after the service, she told others about her "baptism" as the tears of joy literally streamed down her face, beaming with the delight of her experience.

Oh, for the faith of a little child!

On the other hand, a Baptist minister told me recently of the experience of his ten-year-old son who had been saved for some time. The Holy Spirit came upon him, and he "magnified God" for a period of three hours or more, continuing even after he got into bed that night. At the height of his ecstasy his fearful father asked him, "Are you all right, son?"

Completely aware of his family's presence and concern, he stopped just long enough to tearfully reply, "I am all right, Daddy; Oh, I am just so happy. Oh, I love Jesus so much for what He has done for me. He is so wonderful . . . " And his words trailed off into another language with occasional words in English. He was experiencing what Finney called "waves of liquid love."

Whether emotional or quiet, this experience comes at the place of full commitment, yieldedness, and surrender of your heart and life to Christ the King. When you ask, you will receive. Remember Jesus' words, "If ye then, being evil, know how to give good gifts to your children: how much more shall your Heavenly Father give the Holy Spirit to them that ask Him?" (Luke 11:13).

Remain open, then, to anything He has for you.

[2] Andrew Murray, *The Two Covenants* (Chicago: Revell, 1899).

CHAPTER XIV

DON'T LET DISPENSATIONALISM ROB YOU

I spent two years in Pentecost. While I was at Bible school I attended Zion Bible Institute frequently. The more I was around Pentecostals, the more I realized they had something I didn't have, something which was vital to the Christian experience and which I knew I needed.

I left the work I was doing and began preaching in their circles. I conducted vacation Bible schools, attended conferences, directed music, and all the time got more and more hungry for the same experience others were having around me.

Earlier in my life I had had an "upheaval" experience which I now recognize was the baptism of the Holy Spirit. However, since my Pentecostal friends insisted that the only scriptural evidence of the "baptism" was speaking in tongues, I began to doubt my original experience and grew dissatisfied. I became intent on one thing only, speaking in tongues.

In all fairness I need to state that the Pentecostal ministers did not encourage me to seek the gift of tongues. One told me, "It is just like buying a pair of shoes, the tongues come with them." They told me to seek the baptism in the Holy Spirit, believing I could not possibly have received it since I had not spoken in tongues. I grew more and more confused, and yet more and more hungry for this experience with tongues.

One night, after nearly two years of fruitless, defeated living in this confused state, I attended a conference in Worcester, Mass. After the service, during which the gifts were in operation, I went to my room where I was to bunk with another preacher. I lay in bed for some time after the lights were out, trying to think the whole thing through. Gradually I fell into a fitful sleep and dreamed. I dreamed I was in a meeting like the one I had just attended. Many were coming forward for salvation and seeking the power of God in the baptism of the Holy Spirit. As I dealt with them, I, too, began to speak in tongues. I was thrilled. At last I had found what I was seeking. But the bubble burst, for I awoke and realized it was only a dream.

I lay there in bed, listening to the peaceful snoring of the brother across the room. I was heartbroken, and the tears began to flow. I was distressed beyond measure as that horrible sense of defeat and despair settled over me. I had been so close to receiving this gift I had so long sought after, only to have it elude me in a dream. I was broken in spirit.

Then, very quietly yet definitely and clearly, I began speaking to God—only it was in another language. It was so quiet that the one across the tiny room never awoke. But for some time this ecstasy went over and through me as I praised God in words which I could not understand but which I knew were pleasing to Him. I was in the heavenlies. Words fail, even now, almost thirty years later, to describe this magnificent experience of praise and love.

How long the experience lasted I have no idea, but afterward I lay in bed pondering. God had spoken to me—and I to Him. I had an entirely new attitude toward life. The scriptures I had not been willing to face before came alive to me. For the first time in two years I had victory in my soul. It was as if the Lord knew I was about to commit spiritual suicide and allowed me to experience this marvelous gift, even though I had mistakenly been seeking the gift rather than the Giver.

The next morning on the way to the conference, my joy was shattered, however, as I told my co-workers of my experience. The driver, a fellow preacher, was at first so exuberantly happy that he stopped the car, got out and came through the back door to pump my hand and embrace me in rejoicing.

"Praise the Lord, Will," he said. "You've finally received the baptism."

We started on down the road and I felt constrained to

correct his terminology. I told him that I had received the baptism several years before, but that since my Pentecostal friends had said I could not have possibly had this experience without tongues, I had been seeking tongues only. And it was this gift, not the baptism, that I had received the night before.

I can still remember the way his chin dropped in chagrin and disappointment as we drove the rest of the way to the meeting in silence. During the meeting that morning I shared my feelings publicly. It was like a bombshell and nearly wrecked the spirit of the services, although all the brothers present were Pentecostals. However, after the services, at least 200 lay people sided up to me, pumped my hand, and after making sure their pastors were not looking, whispered in my ear, "Brother, we believe like you do."

It was not long after that when I was forced to leave the Pentecostal movement. Although we had much in common, they were not willing to cooperate with me now since I had publicly stated that I believed the baptism of the Holy Spirit did not necessarily have to be initially accompanied with speaking in tongues. Thus for all these years I have been caught in the middle, not accepted by the Pentecostals because my experience didn't fit their theological pattern, and not accepted by the dispensationalists because I had had the experience in the first place.

At this writing I have not spoken in tongues since that experience many years ago. This is not God's fault as I mistakenly said at the time that I had no further desire to use my heavenly language since I felt it had been given just to satisfy my unhealthy desire. Now, however, I plainly see where the Word states emphatically, "I would that ye all speak in tongues," and I can see where tongues edify the believer and the church. It was quite apparent that in the early Corinthian church they were all speaking in tongues and not once did Paul excoriate them for their zeal, nor did he discourage them. Instead he plainly said, "Forbid not to speak in tongues," and that's just about as plain as any commandment that appears in the entire Bible.

Speaking in tongues, especially when given in a message with interpretation, always thrills my soul. I cannot keep the tears back as the Spirit witnesses to me of the reality, the blessing, intended by God through this use in the church. But I thrill just as much when I hear prophecy, or when I witness a discernment of the spirit of God in a meeting that adds to the meeting or routs the enemy of our souls. How wonderful to see and know that God heals, miraculously, instantly, as He did in Paul's case when he received his spiritual baptism. All of these gifts were used in Acts to witness to the reception of the Holy Spirit. And when I am asked by my Pentecostal brethren, "Have you been baptized in the Spirit according to Acts 2:4?" I gratefully answer, "No, but I have been filled according to Acts 8:17."

Out of this personal experience has come new light on the scriptures. Baptism denotes an experience. Certainly, all Christians have the Holy Spirit, but not all have the baptism of the Spirit. Jesus said in Acts 1:5, "For John truly baptized with water; but ye shall be baptized with the Holy Ghost not many days hence." The 120 in the upper room on the Day of Pentecost could not receive the baptism in the Spirit vicariously for me. I have to receive it myself. They did not receive salvation for me, and it is preposterous to say as dispensationalists say, "This was the coming of the Comforter, the Holy Spirit, to all believers on the day of Pentecost." He came *for* all believers, but we were not believers at that time. Therefore we must receive Him now for ourselves.

Dispensationalists say, "I know of no one that is able to drive out demons today." Do they think demons have died of old age? Or do they believe that Jesus didn't know what He was talking about when He said there were demons? Perhaps they think we have grown so smart and sophisticated that demons don't bother us anymore?

Demons exist. They are still around and still subject to the authority of the name of Jesus. The gospel has not lost its power. The name of Jesus has not lost its power. Faith has not lost its power. The Holy Ghost has not lost His power. He still empowers and anoints believers today to drive out demons.

Dispensationalists have a dual standard of requirements for the ministry. They say that those who claim to have power to cast out demons and to pray for the sick and bring healing to tortured bodies should go down and empty the hospitals and psychiatric wards. Yet they believe that God will save sinners today just like He did in Bible days. I ask, "Why don't you go out on the sidewalk and bring salvation to each and every alcoholic, dope addict, homosexual, and other sinner who leans against the sides of your huge church buildings?" Surely God is willing to save them.

However, the answer that comes back is that sinners have to at least cooperate with the gospel. They have to "want" to be saved. Yet they state that this is a poor excuse for our not healing all the sick.

Dispensationalists claim that I Cor. 12:13 is a rank contradiction that tongues are a sign of the baptism in the Spirit. It is not a contradiction. The scripture says, "By one Spirit were we all baptized into one body." The Holy Spirit *has* baptized us into the Body of Christ. But it is Jesus, the Son, who baptizes us in the Holy Spirit.

The dispensationalists use I Cor. 13:8 ("whether there be tongues, they shall cease") to say that tongues have passed away. But that same chapter says, "whether there be knowledge, it shall vanish away." Are the dispensationalists saying that there is no longer any knowledge in the world since there are no more tongues either? It is very clear Paul is talking about the next life and the coming of the Lord when we shall have no need for tongues or prophecy or knowledge or even faith. The only thing that will remain is love.

There need be no wasted years, such as I experienced for nearly two years, seeking something to which I already had access. The scriptures are your guarantee, the Holy Spirit is your guide, God is your Father, and Jesus Christ is your Savior. Can you be more secure than that? He will not give you something bad or something you don't need. He will supply all your needs for witnessing and the ability to live a holy life. He will not give you a gift that will bring reproach upon the Kingdom, for He does all things decently and in order. You can trust Him for all things, and the gifts are yours for the ministry.

"But," someone asks, "I know of many dispensationalist preachers and teachers who believe in and teach the Holy Spirit and the filling of the Holy Spirit. Many of them state that it is something for the Christian after salvation. So, what's the difference?"

The difference is the one thing they lack: miracle. It is at this point most begin to balk, hedge away, and try to explain away what the Bible says. *It is my conviction that this is the reason the church is the laughingstock today.* We have substituted education, ritual, and formality, and we are not willing to face up with a miracle. We seem altogether too willing to settle for something less than the apostles had, even in the face of Acts 2:39.

May I ask you a personal question? Are you satisfied with your experience in the light of the promises of God? I am not asking if you are satisifed with your spiritual life. Even Paul could not say yes to that. But I mean, have you ever asked the Holy Spirit to come into your life and baptize you with power? Have you received the baptism of the Holy Spirit?

Christian, what about it? If you have asked and not received perhaps it is because you have asked amiss. Ask aright. Believing. And the promise shall be yours.

Don't let anyone rob you—not even yourself!

WHERE IS GOD'S POWER!

A city full of churches,
Great preachers, lettered men,
Grand music, choirs and organs;
If these all fail, what then?
Good workers, eager, earnest,
Who labor hour by hour;
But where, oh where, my brother,
Is God's almighty power?

Refinement, education—
They want the very best.
Their plans and schemes are perfect,
They give themselves no rest;
They get the best of talent,
They try their uttermost,
But what we need, my brother,
Is God the Holy Ghost!

It is the Holy Spirit
That quickeneth the soul.
God will not take man-worship,
Nor bow to man's control.
No human innovation,
No skill or worldly art,
Can give a true repentance,
Or break the sinner's heart.

We may have human wisdom,
Grand singing, great success;
There may be fine equipment,
But these things do not bless.
God wants a pure, clean vessel,
Anointed lips and true,
A man filled with the Spirit,
To speak His message through.

—Samuel Stevenson

Epilogue

This morning before church I made the final touches on this manuscript and then reread it entirely.

When I got to the end, reading the poem, I began to weep. I felt an anointing (I don't know what else to call it) that made me raise my hands in praise to Him. This is most unusual for me, for I am not an emotional person by any standard. However, as I raised my hands the praise began to come and flowed from the depths of my soul like rivers of living water, flooding me in waves.

The "feeling" that for the past years has all but disappeared as I have been caught in the web of dispensationalism is returning. And as I pore over these great truths of the scripture, I find myself caught up in emotion, rapture, ecstasy, or whatever you choose to call it. The very truth of the Holy Spirit's work in the Book of Acts, and the knowledge that He is working in exactly the same way today, is literally setting me on fire again. I do not believe I shall ever again be satisifed to work within the "system." Praise God, I am being set free!

SUGGESTED INEXPENSIVE PAPERBACK BOOKS
WHEREVER PAPERBACKS ARE SOLD
OR USE ORDER FORM.

BEN ISRAEL by Arthur Katz
with Jamie Buckingham A503/95¢ -
Odyssey of a modern Jew and
his search for the Messiah.

THE ARMSTRONG ERROR by Charles DeLoach L317/95¢
A reporter investigates Herbert W. Armstrong, The World Tomorrow
broadcast, and the Plain Truth movement.

LOST SHEPHERD by Agnes Sanford L328/95¢
First time in paperback after 7 printings in hard cover. The accounts
of a minister's search for a dynamic ministry and a woman with an
unconventional healing ministry.

AGLOW WITH THE SPIRIT
by Dr. Robert Frost L326/95¢
A scientist shows his spiritual discovery of the baptism in the
Holy Spirit.

WALK IN THE SPIRIT by Michael Harper L319/95¢
There is a place where there is a life to live through the Holy Spirit.

COMING ALIVE by Jamie Buckingham A501/95¢
YOUR NEW LOOK by Jamie Buckingham A502/95¢
COMING ALIVE is a book written for parents and children of pre-
junior high level, presenting a Christian view of sex information.
YOUR NEW LOOK is for the junior high age-level.

15 STEPS OUT by Bob Mumford L106/1.50
Vital questions of practical living considered in relation
to Psalms 120-134.

OVERFLOWING LIFE by Robert Frost L327/1.75
The exciting fulfillment of a spirit-filled life. The experiences
expected after the baptism in the Holy Spirit.

THE SOUL PATROL by Bob Bartlett A500/95¢
A gripping account of teen challenge in Philadelphia, its birth
and outreach to addicts, dropouts and problem youth.

BORN TO BURN by Wendell Wallace with Pat King A508/95¢
Pastor of a multi-racial church
Speaks out on the issues today.

PSEU-DO CHRISTIANS by Dr. Ray Jarman A516/1.00
The dangers of liberal and occult
teaching in lives of Christians and non-Christians.
Dr. Jarman for 50 years was a leader in science of the mind
religions until a dramatic conversion at 70 years of age.

THIS EARTH'S END by Carmen Benson A513/95¢
The Bible contains prophecy telling how this earth
will end. This is a clearly written, easy to understand
explanation of dreams and visions in the New Testament.

JESUS AND ISRAEL by Carmen Benson A514/95¢
The Old Testament revealed through dreams and visions
the future happenings on the earth. An accurate account
of things to come.

WALK IN THE SPIRIT by Michael Harper L319/95¢
Renewal or Revolution — The Church must decide. Some have
discovered a new dimension in living through God's power.

GONE IS SHADOW'S CHILD by Jessie Foy L337/95¢
A moving story of a mother's faith in God for
her son and of a highly effective B10-chemical
treatment called megavitamin in schizophrenia.

SPIRITUAL WARFARE A505/95¢
A practical study on demon oppression and exorcism.
A positive method in freeing the oppressed.

GOD'S JUNKIE by Sonnie Arguinzoni
with Jouinn Ricketts A509/95¢
Introduction by David Wilkerson
A former junkie (his story is in Run Baby Run)
tells of the unique addict church — "Miracles do
happen" by Nicky Cruz.

HEAR MY CONFESSION by Fr. Joseph E. Orsini
L341/95¢ A Roman Catholic priest tells his
personal story of how he discovered the CAtholic
Pentecostal experience.

RUN BABY RUN by Nicky Cruz L-101/95¢
The true story of a gang leader turned crusader.

THE LONELY NOW by Nicky Cruz
with Jamie Buckingham A510/95¢
Nicky answers the questions youth ask.

THE CHALLENGING COUNTERFEIT
by Raphael Gasson L102/95¢
Hidden secrets of spiritualism disclosed by a former medium who tells
how to know the real.

ANGELS OF LIGHT? by Dr. Hobart Freeman A506/95¢
Dr. Freeman reveals the source of power in the popular occult practices
and the deliverance from them.

EMOTIONAL ILLS AND THE CHRISTIAN
by G.J. Guldseth, M.D. A507/95¢
A high percentage of illness is attributed to the psychosomatic.
Dr. Guldseth discusses ways of healing through the Bible.

PRISON TO PRAISE
by Chaplain (LTC) M. Carothers A504/95¢
Revolutionary concepts in achieving remarkable answers to
problems through praise.

THE SPIRIT BADE ME GO
by David du Plessis L-325/95¢
A charismatic journey of one man bringing him before thousands in a
world-wide ecumenical mission for the Holy Spirit.

WISE UP! HOW? by Clinton White L-318/95¢
"I was an alcoholic fourteen years and addicted to drugs. I was set
free. I call it a miracle."